I0086991

THE POWER OF

SUPER GREAT

Finding your happiness and making it stick

LEE E. ELLIS

Copyright © 2018 Lee E. Ellis All rights reserved. No part of this publication may be reproduced, distributed, or transmitted in any form or by any means, including photocopying, recording, or other electronic or mechanical methods, without the prior written permission of the publisher, except in the case of brief quotations embodied in reviews and certain other non-commercial uses permitted by copyright law.

ISBN-13: 978-0-692-05626-4

*I dedicate this book to all those
who struggle to find lasting happiness.
You are not alone in your search for
a resilient positive attitude.*

TABLE OF CONTENTS

Introduction

TOMORROW IS GOING to be the happiest day of your week so far. It's why I wrote this book. We are going to design happiness into your life using simple but scientifically proven ways to interact with your world. Some of the techniques are so readily available to you that it can impact you tomorrow. It really doesn't matter if you are a cubical warrior, a helicopter pilot, or a mom of eight.

Lacking positive feelings, happiness or a sense of well-being seems to be the norm in the world today and it's not your fault. Happiness levels worldwide are declining at an ever-increasing rate. Both "World Happiness Report 2017" and "Happy Planet Index" studies have found a reduction in happiness and the sense of well-being in what most people would view as the strongest economies in the world. How could that possibly be with so many fantastic life-improving devices now available? The survival instinct that we fostered to recognize dangerous situations and anticipate disaster has given us a LASER like focus on tragedy. We couple that focus with the barrage of negative news and social media outrage and we are left with little time or energy to feel happiness in our daily life.

At no time in history has the average human been as busy, distracted and rushed as right now. In this marvelous digital age, we have come to expect nearly instant results. Want to know what the temperature is going to be like in July in Fiji? It used to require a trip to the library in the least. Go further back and you'd get, "What's Fiji?" The access to instant information we have now infects our workplace and our personal lives much more than we have acknowledged. Our bosses want results nearly immediately, and our loved ones want responses only slightly less fast. The constant attention diversions and the must do now emails and text strings have dropped the overall quality of our work and increased the feeling of rush and inadequacy. Our social awareness grows through social media yet our sense of community shrinks. We are badgered daily about every terrible event or shadow of gloom that the news can scrape up. When was the last time you woke with a smile?

It is entirely unrealistic, well at least far too time-consuming, to change the News, the current need for social media, your bosses' project due yesterday attitude and all the other events barring you from a happy life. In this book, I am going to clearly spell out how to set your default to happy. You will wake with a smile and know the day is going to be amazing because you can make it that way. More importantly, those around you will take notice of this example and become happier too, making your life even easier yet. Are you a parent? Share with your children these simple mindsets and tools and watch them grow into happy productive and successful people because happiness is best when shared. You are going to be utterly amazed by how easy it is to change your world for the better. I know, it seems a bit far-fetched, to say the least. I promise I am not going to ask you to vision quest through anything or give your life to any deity; it doesn't even require you to shave your head or take any South American hallucinogenic.

In this book you are going to learn the tools to forgive yourself for those feelings of inadequacy and guilt and move on. How to smile every day and why it is important. How to build resiliency from the negative inputs and thoughts from which we all suffer. How to increase your life's joy every day. How to fill our human need for community even if you don't like your neighbors. Most importantly how to choose happy every single day.

As an obese child, I suffered from the self-esteem and poor self-image that routinely comes with that. Those negative thoughts can eat at you when you are going through puberty. My father, a brilliant man, took me aside and told me I could choose to be happy. I could "tweak" my thoughts this way and that, and if I told myself I was happy, I could be. With his help, my life blossomed into a charmed youthful existence. I ended up with good grades being the prom king (even without being in sports) and marrying the prom queen.

I joined the US army a month later, and my life became prepping for combat. The frequent military induced time apart ended up being too much for the relationship and the happy to bear. I foolishly forgot the lessons of my father. I still had incredible military success, but happy was gone. The rigors that war takes on the mind piled on top of it all, lost friends, lives taken, both enemy and collateral, and time away from my precious children. The struggles after returning were eating at me when those lessons from my childhood came back out of necessity. By the time I was preparing for my second deployment my reputation as an entirely happy person had spread. It changed my outlook, and the change affected those around me for the better. My father's lessons had proven so effective I began researching the science behind happiness and was shocked by how right he had been. From those experiences, I developed the best practices and implemented them in my life for the past five years. They are better than life-improving, and I feel obligated to share his slightly updated wisdom with anyone willing to read or hear. If you believe you can be happy then you have all you will need to make these techniques work and make every part of your life better. Belief or "buy in" that you can be happy is important. Your belief is powerful, that means you are powerful. The proof is in the placebo effect. We see it in science as well. Firm believers in an outcome will see the result they are expecting even when identical experiments do not. This method works, it works so well you are going to share it with everyone you care about. I will present the science behind it. If you want even better results you will share it with your coworkers, them being happy will make your life better. You can wake with a smile; you can have better well-being in your life than you thought possible before. The requirements for happiness are not what you have been lead to believe. You can have reoccurring happiness as a default setting in your life. It doesn't take months to see the results, and you can see them after the first chapter and ESPECIALLY after the second one. The proven health benefits of being happy alone make this a journey worth taking. Let's get started, this is a fun ride down the path to a happier you, after you experience it you will never go back!

But first.

Let's talk about the layout of the chapters. I firmly believe you will get the most out of this book by reading it in its entirety from front to back. However reading is time-consuming and many people don't get a lot out of the typical self-improvement book format: Long story about life, description of authors woes, description of failed attempts, the concept of improvement, then finally how to implement. I am organizing this book a bit differently. I am putting each chapter into this format:

The Concept:

What do I have to do?
How do I do it?
Why should I do It?
My story: (about it working for me).

You can read the first two sections of each chapter and understand what you needed to do. This will appeal to our rushed lives and some people will need little else to make it a success. I, however, am not one of those individuals. I need a bit more, to be convinced some crazy charlatan isn't trying to get one over on me. For those of us that need that the following sections are there. It should also make it far easier to go back and review the heart of each lesson. I like to write notes and highlight the significant bits but am consolidating them for quick reference after the initial reading in this book. I think it will make it a more usable tool toward happiness.

CHAPTER ONE

The Genuine Fake

HAVE YOU EVER noticed that when you smile big, you feel a jolt of happy? Go on, give a large face crinkling smile a try. Doesn't it feel great? I'm smiling as I write this paragraph. It can make a difference in your mood almost immediately. It is a subtle positive change and it's damn hard to feel sad while you're smiling.

Smiling and the act of feeling grateful are two practices that create an improved mood, connectedness and a sense of well-being. They work instantly and have been proven to give lasting and permanent results when practiced on a regular basis. In this chapter, I will discuss the best ways of committing to smiling and showing gratitude on a daily basis. I will also show how they can permanently increase your happiness level.

The Concept:

Smiling will make you happier. It really is that simple. There is considerable scientific evidence, that we will discuss later, proving it works. It might even seem like a very silly idea at first or that it is too simple a concept. It works, it is easy and you have nothing to lose by trying.

In this chapter I am going to show you simple strategies that will have you smiling more and gaining all the benefits that it provides. By adding gratitude to your smile as a daily practice you will create and notice more opportunities throughout your day, resulting in happier more fulfilling days.

What do you have to do?

There are several things that you need to understand about smiling before you can benefit from the most powerful gesture in the world. First, there are two common types of smile. The first type is the social smile. This is often used by adults. It requires that you only turn up the sides of your mouth. This is also called a non-Duchenne smile named after the French neurologist Guillaume Duchenne, who studied emotional expression by stimulating various facial muscles with electrical currents. Fortunately for us, we don't have to electrocute your face to study this effect hand.

The social (or Non-Duchenne) smile is used by adults who greet one another in passing and those who are not known personally to us, such as sales clerks. It is the most common smile used during the day. There isn't much benefit to using that particular type of smile, other than being polite. It is a worthwhile practice but not the smile we need to create the happiness we are after. The genuine smile (Duchenne smile) is the smile I will be focusing on and teaching you to build into your daily routine. It involves not just the mouth but also the eyes. This makes it a full-face smile. We will explore the mechanics of both types of smiles in the next section. It is important to know that the genuine smile (Duchenne smile) can be faked. Even when forced you still enjoy all of the positive benefits, as if it were a result of real positive emotions. The 'fake-genuine' smile sounds hilariously ironic, but it works and is an instant pick-me-up.

Another important concept of happiness is gratitude. When you practice gratitude, you cannot help but smile. When you are grateful, even for the small things in life, you automatically smile. The most thorough explanation I have read about gratitude is by Harvard University Medical School:

"Gratitude-a thankful appreciation for what an individual receives, whether tangible or intangible. With gratitude, people acknowledge the goodness in their lives. As a result, gratitude also helps people connect to something larger than themselves as individuals – whether to other people, nature, or a higher power."

Using this description of gratitude helps us to consider a broad range of things or feelings that we can feel gratitude for. You should not confuse expressing gratitude, with actually feeling it. You must make that internal connection from noticing to feeling to gain the full benefit of gratitude.

How do I do it?

An amazing attribute of children is the amount of time that they spend smiling. With modern 3-D ultrasound we can see babies smiling before they are even born and keep on smiling until late adolescence. During this time, you go from smiling over four hundred times a day to about twenty times a day as you reach adulthood. Worst of all, most of those smiles as an adult are not even genuine smiles. They are just a social nod to other people who you pass throughout your day. It's been so long since smiling was a routine element in our lives that most of us don't even remember how amazing it can be to smile often or how the mechanics of smiling work.

Why do we stop smiling as much as we did as children? There are too many explanations to list them all. Let's look at a couple of the main reasons adults give when asked. Admittedly most are ridiculous even though they still are squashing most of our smiles. Here are some of the excuses that people give for not smiling:

1) Smiling makes you look weak: You could be seen as a pushover. Just because you appear happy, you will say 'yes' to everything and anything. Wrong! Just because you are smiling, doesn't mean that 'yes' has to be your answer. I am a firm believer in "no" as a life improving and self-empowering word. I don't even have to stop smiling to say the word 'no', and I rarely do.

2) I'm a man, and it socially unacceptable to smile too much: On average, men smile 50% less than women.

Men are supposed to be tough and manly. Therefore, an outward, positive expression of emotion such as smiling, does not fit into the personification of masculinity. This is a cultural problem that has been ingrained into the brains of men for too many years. It is a ridiculous, outdated concept that needs to be challenged. It is hampering many men from being truly happy. I am a man. I smile because I can't contain the joy in my life. Not convincing enough for you? Look at the richest and most powerful men in the world. Most of them are prolific smilers. Here are a few examples:

Richard Branson   Warren Buffet   Michael Jordan

3) I have a bad smile or my teeth aren't straight: This is one of my own excuses. It is the reason why I squashed a bunch of happiness out of my life during my youth. I do not have the straightest teeth. I also love, love, love tea which is not conducive with a Hollywood smile. Even though my teeth are not perfect, the #1 compliment that I receive is "Lee, you have an amazing smile!"

A beaming smile can compensate for almost any physical imperfection you may feel about your smile. We are going to look at the way you smile and how you can tweak a good one (all genuine smiles are good without exception) into an amazing show-stopping powerhouse of happiness. Let's take a look at a few world leaders who use both a genuine smile and a socially acceptable smile to help us learn the difference.

GENUINE	SOCIAL
President Obama's genuine smile. Full wrinkles around the eyes and round cheeks	President Obama's social smile. Notice the lack of lines around the eyes and the cheeks aren't fully rounded
President Putin's genuine smile	President Putin's social smile

GENUINE	SOCIAL
President Xi Jinping's genuine smile	President Xi Jinping's social smile
Prime Minister Trudeau's genuine smile	Prime Minister Trudeau's social smile

Did you notice anything in yourself as you looked at the pictures? Did you also smile when you looked at the genuine photos?

Let's take a look now at your smile and see if we can make improvements. Here are several tips to making your smile look great and have a positive impact on others.

1. **You'll need a mirror for this exercise.** When I first started practicing smiling it seemed silly to me. However, it is now something that I love to do every morning. I admit it does bring out a lot of hilarity.

Laughing at yourself, for practicing such a simple task, is a great way to bring out your genuine, amazing smile.

The real key to success, while practicing in front of the mirror, is to stop being so picky with yourself. You will never allow yourself to see your smile as perfect because we are naturally more critical of ourselves. Let it go my friend. You have a smile that is dying to break out. It is now time to set that monster free. No one, other than your dentist, is going to think to themselves that your smile isn't perfect because of that chipped, crooked, or discolored tooth.

Look in the mirror and try out a social smile like the ones we saw in the pictures above. Notice the non-emotional eyes and the overly stiff lips. Think about how you feel when you place a social smile on your face. There might be a little happiness in there (because as I've explained – you can't help but be happy when you smile), but it's not all consuming or intense, is it?

You should now go all out and really smile. Let the smile touch every part of your face. Your cheeks should start to rise and your eyes will instinctively close a little, as your cheeks push upwards. This is when the dreaded crow feet appear. Let me tell you a secret. This is the most endearing part of you. The lines that surround your eyes are, in fact, attractive. They make you appear real and full of life. Some people call them laugh lines because they are a positive and not a negative part of you. It is the western world that judges these perfectly, natural wrinkles as a bad thing. Have you ever seen a person who has had Botox smile? It just doesn't look right. It's because they have no laugh lines and without those beautiful crinkly, wrinkles, the smile is just not a smile. If you don't believe me, take a look at a child when they are truly smiling. They also have beautiful wrinkles around their eyes. It is a natural part of a human smile.

Are you smiling? You should remember not to be overly critical. A head tilt is a good idea. "The Like Switch" by Jack Schafer and Marvin Karlins talks about the slight tilt of the head being universal human body language to indicate friendliness. Keeping your head stiff and upright is an indication of dominance. This is weird but true. I had never noticed the head tilt before. However, now it is a constant part of my smiling greeting.

You will need to work on your smile a few minutes every morning until you perfect it. This doesn't mean that you to wait to use your smile until you feel it's perfect. Over the next few days, practice on everyone. It will get better every time you whip it out. Every time you would have just given a social smile to someone, I want you to bring out the real deal. Slap that stranger with a grin he or she will notice.

2. **When was the last time you saw a loved one who lives far away?** Remember that feeling? Keep that feeling in your mind. When you need to smile, bring

the feeling out and let it fuel your smile. It will help you give someone an awesome smile. It also is a good opportunity to feel gratitude for those people and the good times in your life. Use those memories to help you smile big throughout your day, even when you would normally not be smiling. You need to do this several times a day. This will help with the last step to an amazing smile.

3. **You need to become comfortable with your smile.** You should feel great about it! If you haven't been smiling much lately you might still feel uncomfortable, it might take a bit longer to feel great about it. At most it should only be a day or two. Once people start responding and smiling back at you you will know you have nailed it. The goal is for you to not feel awkward or out of place smiling.

Let's recap: Find your best smile. Use those happy memories to produce more genuine heartfelt smiles throughout your day. Use your smile over and over again, until it feels comfortable on your face. Once it does, you will have the best and most versatile tool you will ever have in your life. No Sham-Wow or Slap Chop will ever compete with it.

To reach smiling perfection, you must take this tool out of the shed and use it a lot. My favorite way to do this is what I call the smile game. In both Harvard University and University of Michigan studies about the smile, which I will discuss in the next section, they discovered that we naturally imitate the smile given to us by another. We reflect it almost exactly as it is given to us in every situation. Mirroring helps us to determine if the smile we are receiving is genuine.

Due to this natural mirroring effect, if you smile the person you smile at will mimic that same expression back to you. It is the science behind the smiling game. People view those with social non-genuine smiles as suspicious and untrustworthy. This is one of the reasons that we need to practice our genuine smile.

I still do the following exercise/game routinely during the day. When you are commuting, or out and about, look any person that you pass in the eye and give them your best smile. You can even do this with strangers. Although it might seem weird, the goal is to see if they smile back. Don't stare! Just glance over at them and hit them with your magic. You would think that in the bigger cities it wouldn't work at all. However, it is a natural human reaction to smile back when you are smiled at. Neuroscientist Marco Lacoboni explains it like this, "When I see you smiling, my mirror neurons for smiling fire up, too, initiating a cascade of neural activity that evokes the feeling we typically associate with a smile. I don't need to make any inference on what you are feeling, I experience immediately and effortlessly (in a milder form, of course) what you are experiencing."

Because of those mirror neurons you are going to get a lot of people to smile back. When I smiled at people in Seoul, I had about 50% of the people smile back at me. In Bangkok, it worked nearly every time. In Denver it worked almost every time, while in Chicago it was less than half. Why your success in different locations varies is up to you to decide. Even in the places you don't get your full smile back, you will see people catching themselves to prevent it. They have to fight their neural mirror response.

The truly tough spots I've found are small towns in the United States. The people you know will see your smile and be compelled to talk to you. It feels like a green light for them to come up and speak to you- the happy person. We just can't help ourselves. The success rate you get doesn't matter. However, it is still fun to track it. What is important is that you are out there practicing the smile and collecting the many benefits. We will discuss the list of benefits from smiling at the end of this chapter. There is a bonus. You get to spread happiness to all those that returned your smile, and they get all the same benefits you do from it. It could be just the boost someone else needs to make their day. You don't have to play The Smile Game. Once you start, you will have a hard time not playing it everywhere.

Gratitude

"Cultivate the habit of being grateful for every good thing that comes to you, and to give thanks continuously. And because all things have contributed to your advancement, you should include all things in your gratitude."
– Ralph Waldo Emerson

Gratitude is another extremely powerful yet simple thing we can do in our lives to make it better. The first step is to acknowledge that there is goodness in your life, no matter how small. You might be experiencing depression or you might believe there is little goodness in your life. I assure you there is good in your life if you take the time to look for it, even if it's for the bed you sleep in or the food you have, this gratitude can be a spark of happiness in your life.

How we find gratitude in our lives is relatively easy. Just refer to Ralph Waldo Emerson's quote. You can and should be grateful for all of the good things that come up in your life. Because "ALL THINGS have contributed to your advancement," and that includes our failures. I have learned more and even avoided tragedy, due to failures in my life. I learned about the glory of the burnt marshmallow by sucking on my singed fingers, which were covered with volcanic magma hot marshmallow. It was tasty and painful. I would not have tried them that black any other way. Thank you flaming sugar goo for the lessons of being careful and being delicious!

It is that simple. The list of things to feel truly grateful for is plentiful. You just need to look. If you've traveled outside the U.S., you may know that clean, and reliable drinking water is something that is worth gratitude. The warm bed and the blanket, the freedom to vote, or to sing and dance are all worthy targets that not all of us are allowed to do. I am even grateful that no one can hear me sing in the shower!!

The second step of gratitude is recognizing that sometimes the reason for being grateful comes from outside yourself. I am thankful that there are apples. I love them and am grateful that my neighbor left some on my doorstep.

Reasons like that or even higher spiritual reasons all work for this process. Once you pick your thing to be grateful for, you need to say thanks for it and MEAN it. Let the feeling of being grateful touch you. You should do it at least once a day. I get started in the morning. There will be plenty of things that happen to you or around you, that will warrant gratitude by the end of your day. Some people like to practice gratitude just before they go to bed. I will discuss a great location to place that gratitude in a later chapter, when we look at an easy daily routine to cultivate a happier life. But don't wait until you get there, be thankful for something right now.

Why should I do it?

There have been many studies about smiling and its health benefits. They are awe-inspiring. Get ready to smile my friends because the results are going to inspire you. For starters, smiling stimulates our brain's reward mechanisms like eating a bar of chocolate does, but on a far grander scale.

A U.K. study used an electromagnetic brain scan machine and a heart-rate monitor to create "mood-boosting values" from different stimuli. They discovered that one smile provides the same level of neural stimulation as up to 2,000 chocolate bars. That's just from ONE smile! You could wave goodbye to cavities and the 47,000 calories it would cost you to eat that much, to get the same results as a smile.

Studies also found that smiling is as stimulating as receiving £16,000 in cash which is $25,000 U.S dollars. This result is a little suspicious, primarily because if someone handed me £16,000 I would get both the cash and a huge smile. It would be like doubling the benefit!

Smiling is one of the first instincts we have as humans. Since the use of the 3-D ultrasound, parents have started seeing their preborn babies smiling. They smile in reaction to hearing their mother's voice or any other number of stimuli. The expression of joy and happiness is the first definable gesture that we all make. This tells us a lot more about our nature than anything else. We know how to be happy in the womb. All that we have to do now is remember this innate ability.

From before birth, children smile and continue to do so. Children produce genuine smiles around 400 times a day compared to the 20 or so that an adult will muster. The smiles start to fade as we reach adolescence and then hit rock bottom when we are in our early twenties. I do not want this to happen to my children. I am teaching them to smile big and often.

Have you ever noticed how much happier you feel around playing children? I admit I can't stop smiling around them myself. There is a scientific reason why it's hard to stop. It turns out that a genuine smile, with the contracting of the muscles around the mouth and eyes, sends a signal to the brain that trips the reward mechanisms in body. The brain and body then get a hit of the endorphins, oxytocin, serotonin, and dopamine sending a big happy smile to your lips. This amazing biochemical reaction improves your immune system, blood pressure, reaction to stress, balance, self-control and our sense of well-being. All from a genuine smile, which then makes you feel like smiling more. It's a great, big, loop of joy, revel in it.

Smiling is a behavior. We will be looking at the practice of cognitive behavior therapy (CBT) throughout the book as it relates to living a happier life. When we do we can see additional benefits from the behavior of smiling. These are benefits that have a huge impact on our overall feelings of happiness. I will discuss a little more about CBT in the next few chapters. In it's simplest here is how it works. In CBT there is a triangle of core attributes that affect your moods and daily life. They are: your Behaviors, Thoughts and Emotions. They are all closely linked. Your sad/angry/happy emotions change your thought patterns. That has an effect on your behavior, which reinforces your emotions. Have you ever gotten into a "funk" and had a hard time getting out of it? I have. The CBT triangle helps explain the link and why that funk can be so hard to shake off. For instance, you yell at the coffee clerk. It makes you feel guilty and upset. Your thoughts are now more likely to be negative and linger on the other inadequacies of your day. This makes you physically move slower, which reinforces the gloomy emotions and fuels self-anger for not accomplishing enough during your day. This can lead to you being irritable and angry towards others.

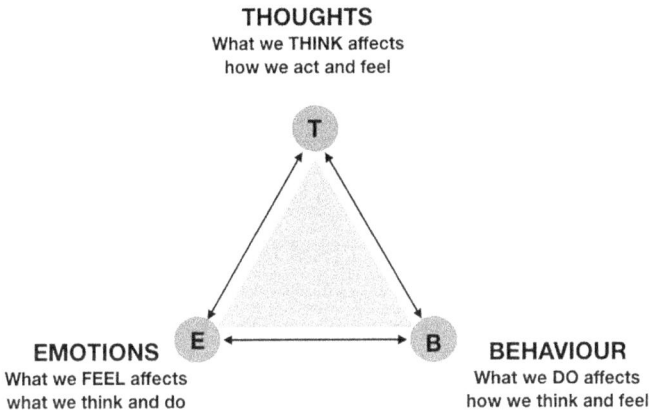

THOUGHTS
What we THINK affects
how we act and feel

T

EMOTIONS   E   B   **BEHAVIOUR**
What we FEEL affects   What we DO affects
what we think and do   how we think and feel

Smiling is a powerful behavior. It affects both your thoughts and your emotions. It is more powerful than most people might think. As discussed before, our brain is hardwired to give us an emotional uplift from the act of smiling. It doesn't matter if it is a fake smile or a real smile. Our brain releases the same positive chemical cocktail and applies the emotional jolt of joy to our system. That is a lot of power for just one behavior.

When you smile, you get the behavior and emotional bonus on top of it. It doesn't take much else to also drag your thoughts to a more positive place. I want you to think about what that means to us as humans. We smile before we are even born. Smiling is also the most powerful behavior that we participate in and is hardwired to bring joy and health. We have been purposely built to be happy whether it is through evolution or design. Smiling frequently has even been shown to affect other portions of the brain. It changes the physical pathways in the mind and builds new connections. Those changes result in an increase in the amount of smiles you produce and in the boost you get from each one. It's like our subconscious is keeping track of the genuine and fake smiles that you have every day. The increased frequency begins to make smiling a more common occurrence on its own. It changes how we view the very world around us, by making our outlook more positive. That positive outlook changes the way we perceive the events and people we interact with daily.

Teaching someone to genuinely smile more is like handing them the perfect tool to achieve happiness. It is the one that is meant for this job. Even though I don't wish to sound like an infomercial salesman, let's look at other free bonuses you'll get when you buy into the smiling more!

What else can this facial miracle produce for you? A recent study by the University of Kansas, published in "Psychological Science" found that when people smiled, they experienced large reductions in heart rates and other body stress indicators. They also observed that smilers recovered from stressful events much more rapidly than the control group. The heart rate implications of reduced stress have supported other studies that also reported a reduction in cortisol, a known chemical related to stress levels. The heart seems to love a smile as much as the rest of us.

The Kansas study also observed reduced levels of discomfort, aches and pains, for smilers compared to non-smilers. However, they made no conclusions about that part of their study, since it was not their main focus. Although discomfort is difficult to judge and subjective, the University still thought it was important enough to mention.

In addition to these compelling reasons to start smiling as much as possible, there are also outward reasons. Imagine what it would be like going to your office and smiling every day. It would be great if you chose to smile big at people and they return it as a response. Your smile will help improve their mood and start rewiring their brain to also experience more smiles and positivity. This lifts spirits and causes even more smiles that make the group both happier and healthier. After only a few weeks, you have created a better working environment for everyone.

Both men and women rate people who are genuinely smiling to be more attractive than if that same individual was not smiling. They also, unsurprisingly, find them to be more approachable and are more likely to have positive feelings about an encounter with someone who is smiling.

There is even a link between smilers and long life and success. In the famous "Yearbook study", high school yearbook photos of women were examined. They found that genuine smilers reported much happier lives and had lived longer and claimed to have less troubled times. The study has been repeated several times all with the same results. On average, those high school students with big bright smiles, lived much happier, longer lives. The studies did not examine the causes of longer life or why they had been happier. However, the results have been the same in all similar studies.

A similar, famous study is the baseball card study. It found that the bigger the player's smile on the card, the longer the length of the player's life. Big smilers averaged seven years longer life. It was no surprise that they also reported better health throughout their life.

Gratitude doesn't quite have the number of studies on it that the smile does. However, there are compelling reasons to start engaging in this practice. The act of feeling gratitude for someone else's actions connects us to the community as a whole. Showing gratitude often helps us in our search for the positive things in life. Gratitude has been very important influential throughout history. Roman politician Marcus Tullius Cicero urged us to seek it saying, "Gratitude is not only the greatest of virtues, but the parent of all the others." It is a builder of strong teams, the mender of hurtful relations and a balm for overworked employees.

Recently published studies have found a significant connection to self and being in the present in those who frequently express gratitude. Robert Emmons, Ph.D., a Professor of Psychology at UC Davis in California, has been studying the effects of gratitude in over 1,000 people. The participants ranged from eight to eighty and were split into two separate groups. One group journaled about five "gifts" they were grateful for every day and the other group journaled about five "hassles" they had experienced. Emmons found both physical and social benefits in those that journaled about gratitude, which included a 25% improvement in overall health and well-being, compared with the group that focused on what had gone wrong each day. He found that those who kept a gratitude journal on a daily/weekly basis exercised more regularly, reported fewer physical symptoms, felt better about their lives as a whole and were more optimistic about the upcoming week, compared to those who recorded hassles or neutral life events. They also took fewer sick days off. This is a huge difference for such a minimal amount of effort which takes only a few moments each day. We will talk more about journaling later in the book as it can be a powerful tool in your life.

My Story:

I spent over twenty-one years as a professional soldier in the U.S. Army. Toward the end of my career, I was assigned as a Master Gunner and was attached to the unit's planning section, called the S-3's shop. The head of the shop was a Major and is called the S-3. He was the lead planner for all the operations in the unit. This particular S-3 was extremely hard to deal with. He was also brilliant at his job as a planner. He was the perfect vision of what most people think of as an army officer, but way shorter!

The good Major got up an hour earlier than necessary to do extra physical training before regular army physical training. He would then work a mere sixteen-hour day. He would sometimes break for a meal but mostly ate at his desk while working. This kind of dedication doesn't always mean that an officer will be a hard to work for. However, in this case, he expected most of his shop to follow a similar schedule. The shop adopted the name "The Pit". It was short for "The Pit, where all your hopes and dreams come to die, especially on weekends."

I got my desk in the pit. After working there a few weeks, it was brutally apparent that everyone was unhappy all of the time. This negativity was also spilling over into our off time. Unhappy days were followed by unhappy, long working nights. By this point in my life, I was immune to such gloom. I started smiling more and more purposely. I thanked people profusely even for the smallest of tasks. The days when people were the most negative, were the days when I smiled the most and thanked people the loudest. People couldn't help themselves. They smiled back. Some of them got irritated with me for smiling and occasionally joking with them. Others thought it was ridiculous to thank someone for doing their job. "How can this son of a bitch smile after a sixteen-hour day in the pit?" I heard this kind of comment regularly. Every time I got the chance, I would whip out my best grin. The gloomier the person that approached me was, the bigger the smile I gave them. I brought in cookies and cupcakes as a thank you. I also started joking and renaming "The Pit". I called it the Cuddle Dungeon and The Happy Pony Rainbow Ranch anything to break up the idea of it being so negative. Whenever anyone asked me how I was, I'd tell them the truth "I'm super great!" or "Fan-tabulous!" As a result, the mood in the shop brightened.

Within a few weeks, I was no longer the only smiler. I then stopped being the only person who was doing 'super great'. The workflow increased as people worked better with each other and the office wasn't as gloomy. The Major even brightened up a bit and joked about it all. The work environment was a transformed place and "The Pit" was no longer.

In a little over a month, the group in the S-3 shop were still working ridiculously long hours under a lightened but tyrannical leader. However, they were now a group of smiling officers. I had succeeded in helping bring a more positive feel to our working lives.

Smiling is infectious and addictive. Gratitude is life-enhancing. For a while, I was the dealer to all of those in the pit, but soon they were pushing it out to each other. Since it was so bad, it was easy for me to have a positive impact. I am lucky to have worked there, even when it wasn't the most pleasant place to be. I had help in 'The Pit' because the soldiers were all outstanding in their own fields. They all craved a bit more happiness, including the Major. It turns out that he has an amazing smile himself.

CHAPTER TWO

Forgiving Yourself and Others

"Be courageous enough to forgive yourself;
never forget to be compassionate to yourself."
– Debasish Mridha

The Concept

HARBORING NEGATIVE THOUGHTS and feelings about yourself, your job and your performance, all prevent you from becoming a consistently happy person. Forgiving others and yourself is more beneficial to you than harboring negative feelings. Accepting who you are and your situation, is a fundamental step in building the foundation of happiness for your life.

Negative feelings include anxiety, guilt, nonproductive stress, doubt, worry, poor self-image, sense of inadequacy, anger, regret, etc.

What do you have to do?

Let go of all the negative emotions and beliefs about yourself, your position and about those in your life. You will then be able to see the truth of where you currently are. This is great news, since life is rarely as bad as you think it is while you are letting these negative emotions and thoughts skew your point of view.

When we walk around consumed by thoughts of current and past inadequacies, we create more anxiety, stress, doubt, regret and other nonproductive feeling. These thoughts can include: I have too many belly rolls, I have bad teeth, I am not smart enough, my job sucks and my last presentation at work was terrible. This will leave you with anxiety and negativity that will destroy your happiness and your health.

Negative thoughts about other people can also make you feel bad. These thoughts include: my co-worker is lazy, he is always hindering me, takes credit from me and never makes a fresh pot of coffee. This thought process harms us in the short term and also creates fertile ground for greater worries and more negative emotions. The "Not smart enough" thoughts are combined with the "my job sucks" thoughts. Pretty soon we have a party in our heads with other thoughts such as "This is the best I can do," "I can't start over," "I hate my job," and "I'm too dumb to get promoted." This problem quickly gets out of hand and can be worse than you think.

Negative thoughts can like these affect the way we view our environment and seem to attract negative life events. As a result, we change our outlook from finding opportunities to being devastated by change. They also modify the way that others see us. Someone who is hard to work with because of a negative self-image, can drag down a group and quickly be excluded from it, especially if they do not keep their negativity in check.

Holding others in contempt for past errors damages ourselves even more than it does them. Even if you manage to conceal hurtful feelings for a while, they taint your outlook and may eventually slip out in unexpected ways. Don't waste time trying to hide your hostile feelings. It results in poor performance and makes you expend too much precious energy. Individuals who are always making negative comments, are noticed throughout an organization. As a result, that big promotion you've earned could be given to a less qualified but more positive person, I have seen it happen. Management wants to work with a self-confident person who is easy to get along with. They want to work with the person who smiles, even when their desk is on fire. It is not that they don't appreciate your work or performance. It is only human nature to want to work with pleasant people. They see upbeat people in positive light so it becomes easy for them to envision that kind of person making positive changes to their organization. It helps to create a harmonious workplace and increases productivity. We are going to work on YOU and fostering a great reputation in a later chapter but we must tackle this task of getting rid of some negative emotions and thoughts first.

How Can I Do It?

I do not understand why so many people believe for-giveness requires a certain amount of suffering. Thank-fully knowing that answer isn't a requirement to forgive-ness, only knowing that it isn't true is. You are a great person, I know it and you deserve to live your best possi-ble life! Without a solid self-image, based on acceptance, you can't create lasting happiness. If you can't accept your flaws, weaknesses and imperfections, then you will never be happy. Your mental perception of who you are, influ-ences every thought and action in your life. By accepting I do not mean resign to being. Truthful identification of a flaw is the first step to improving yourself. You have to stop seeing yourself as an imperfect, unworthy, human being. You are a good person. The mistakes you have made along the way have helped you to grow and to develop into the person you are today.

However, your mistakes do not define you. Don't be one of the people who punish themselves for their per-ceived flaws whether they be internal or purely physical.

I've been unhappy with my outer-self before so understand how hard that struggle can be. When the outside world is viewing you as physically different, it is harder to overcome the doubts and worries. Issues such as being overweight or underweight, having bad com-plexion, or bad posture can be viewed negatively by other people and it changes the way they interact with us. Even something as minor as a bad hair day, can change how the world treats us. With such minor things changing the way the world treats us imagine the difficulties those with physical disabilities face every day. It's not fair but if I were to claim differently, then I would be robbing you of the benefits that you will enjoy from overcoming these obstacles in your life. You CAN do it. I know that you can.

It's important when dealing with outward differences to realize that even if you can change those aspects about yourself, you do not need to change them to be happy. You should forgive yourself for any negative feelings or thoughts you have about your differences. Accepting who you are right now will remove much of the guilt and negative feelings you are harboring. Once you have forgiven and accepted who you are, it is much easier to identify the realistic actions you can take and implement the changes that you want in your life. This includes more than just learning to be happy. It will affect everything in your life. It also makes it much easier to recognize and ignore negative attention from the outside world. When you are subjected to negativity, you shouldn't react by reflecting it back even though that is our natural instinct. It is better to just smile and let it wash by you. This approach makes a positive impression and usually neutralizes the offender. It will also be much more difficult to achieve happiness, if you start out reacting negatively every time you encounter those negative people. Throw them off balance by flashing the amazing smile at them. A flustered negative person is a bonus to anyone's day!

It is going to be necessary to forgive complete strangers who mistreat you and do so in a positive manner. The difference:

"I forgive you for upsetting me because you are just an insensitive jerk."

vs.

"I forgive you for upsetting me because you still don't see how amazing I am and I know you are missing out because of it."

It can be a tough mental shift, but it is worth it. You don't need to make either of these statements to the offending person, just use it as a way to mentally filter their unacceptable behavior. If we allow the random rude or insensitive person to upset us then we are essentially handing them power over us. Those are the last kind of people we want to have any say in how our day is, or how we feel about ourselves. It's not always easy to forgive them but doing so releases the power hold over you. Forgive them, brush their insensitive comments from your shoulder and claim the power over choosing your mood and reaction. It's quite empowering.

It is easy to explain how to forgive yourself. Actually forgiving yourself and accepting your current situation is the greatest obstacle to achieving happiness. Acknowledging that we have made mistakes, learning from them, and moving on, needs to become a habit that doesn't require any willpower. The goal is for it to become another natural habit where you accept that you are an imperfect but improving person. It is perfectly alright to not be in ideal physical shape, to not have the job you want, or to not be with the perfect partner. It is also OK if you do not know how to fix those things.

If you accept how you are and where you are, it will shine a new light on the path you need to help you to get to where you want to be. There is even better news, getting to where you want to be isn't going to be as difficult as you've been telling yourself. Small changes can make huge improvements given the right attitude and patience. For instance, walking the stairs or for 20 minutes a day is a great start to better fitness. It will be the first steps to getting your ideal body and also give you added energy. There are jobs available for amazing people like you with the skills that you have. The man/woman of your dreams is also out there looking for you. When you have confidence and a positive self-image, others will see it too. This will make job hunting, relationship building, and personal development even easier.

When you accept and learn to love yourself, it enables and encourages others to do the same. If you want to learn acceptance as well as happiness, you have picked up the right book. I am going to list a couple of things that I have found helpful for forgiving yourself.

- The most important thing to understand about acceptance and forgiveness is that you have to believe they will work. Your belief can be very powerful. That is why it is essential for you to accept and forgive yourself. If you don't accept your current situation, you will not have a strong foundation for change. If you are consumed with regret and guilt and don't forgive yourself, it will result in many negative feelings that will keep you from achieving happiness.

• You must first identify the issue, so you can determine what is making you feel upset about the situation. Once you know that, figuring out the lesson you were meant to learn is easy. The lesson is never self-deprecating. If you feel that way, it devalues you and the lesson. There is a difference between "It happened because I am an idiot," vs. "It happened because I made a specific mistake." Once you've identified the lesson, I find it helpful to say it out loud. This brings it into the physical world. After this smile, you've just become a better, improved person. You must accept that the event is unalterable and in the past, where it requires none of your energy. You should then forgive yourself for the mistake. The lesson is learned, it has served its purpose in your life.

• Say this aloud:

"I deserve forgiveness for all the things I have been holding on to. I forgive me."

It seems overly simple, but it works. You should say it loud and proud a couple of times a day, preferably as you look into a mirror. This helps to not only get it through to your subconscious mind but also gives it a physical feel. However, there is a disclaimer: When you do this exercise, those nagging negative thoughts are going to rear their ugly heads. If they do, you should say something like this:

> *"I deserve forgiveness for all the things I have been holding on to. I forgive me."*

> *Your mind: Whoa, buddy! What about that time you pushed your sister off the swing and she broke her arm?*

Your response,

> *"Yes, it was cruel, I didn't mean for her to be hurt that badly, but she was. I am a better person now, and I forgive me."*

Then move on with your day.

There might be things that pop up. If they do, acknowledge them, forgive yourself and let it go. If they don't pop up, there is no need to dig around in your mind looking for stuff to drag up, you should just move on with your day. After a few days, you may start to notice uncomfortable or upsetting thoughts popping up during your day. This is also good. You can forgive yourself for those as well.

You need to be careful. These thoughts are an attempt by your brain to return to its old negative ways where it has become comfortable. We are changing your patterns of thought and humans are habit driven, so your mind will drift back to its negative pattern when not watched carefully. We need to change those habits to acknowledge and release negative emotions. When they do surface, you should acknowledge them and forgive yourself. It is important to practice releasing these emotions, and the thoughts that go with them, just like you would train for anything else. You shouldn't worry if you find this to be difficult. Do not be too hard on yourself. It takes practice. Your brain probably isn't going to want to cooperate yet. It will take some willpower and determination to overcome this. You should remember that this is a healing exercise. It will heal you but you must be patient. This can be an emotional roller coaster because the events associated with guilt and remorse are strong. You can allow yourself to feel that remorse. However, you must then forgive yourself. Think of something positive related to that event, then feel gratitude for the lesson you learned or something positive that resulted from it.

During your self-forgiveness journey, you might want to apologize to someone. This helps relieve us of the guilt we feel for our behavior and is much easier than forgiving ourselves. We hold ourselves to a much harder, often unrealistic standard than we do others. Be careful of unrealistic standards in your life both past and present. They can leave us feeling bad about ourselves for years. Identifying these unrealistic views will help absolve ourselves from the guilt and upset. We need to make an honest assessment of ourselves, accept it and move on. You can still apologize, if you feel it is necessary. My preference is to apologize in person or by a call, but a text message will do in a pinch. You must do what feels right for you. You can post it, tweet it, text it, or send a postcard (they still have those), letter or email. I've even apologized to a person, even though I could not locate him. I just apologized out loud and believed it would get to him somehow.

Send a heartfelt apology to whomever needs it and then let it go. You do not need their forgiveness, although it is always nice to have it. As soon as you send your apology, forgive yourself. This might seem like a long road, but it isn't. Once you start forgiving yourself, the pace will quicken. In less than a week, you will notice the difference. Forgiving yourself in this way helps you to develop a habit that is great for your overall health. Acknowledging and then releasing the emotions and ideas that you need to forgive yourself for, is the same process used for recognizing and releasing other negative emotions. It also helps to brush aside intruding and unhelpful thoughts. This technique can help you to reduce anxiety, fear, stress and doubt. It will clear your mind to make room for helpful, productive ideas. It will help you to assess your condition and circumstances honestly and accept them. The result of this process is that you will have a stronger sense than ever before on how to become a better happier you.

Visualization:

Visualization is a mental tool which accesses the imagination to realize all aspects of an object, action or outcome. If you watch TV or video, it is likely that you are being bombarded by the visualization technique every day. I am sure that you have seen images of others having fun and experiencing joy, but only when taking drug X or drinking substance Y. Advertisers use images to promote positive emotions and then linking them to their product. It is an extremely effective tool. They show you beautiful beaches and amazing parties with their product in the image. Since they repeatedly play the commercials, the beautiful beach never loses its appeal. It doesn't take many showings for you to associate the desire to go to that beach or party with their product. They have created a visualization for you of what the perfect beach or party looks like. The next time you go to the beach or a party, you will likely grab their product to complete that image. If you can't go, then you may just purchase the product so that you can get a small piece of that dream. The amazing thing is that the same process that works for them, also works for you only much better. When you create the right image, all of its components are for your improvement and for reaching your own goals. It takes effort to build visualization into a useful tool. You must create the image of a near perfect you and then play it in your head a few times a day. Visualization can be a very useful technique, it takes only a few seconds once you start using it and is very versatile for different goals. The visualization techniques don't change much, even when the purpose you are using them for does.

The next section presents a guide to the essentials of visualization. It is important to try to get the most detailed image possible from your imagination. Let's get started.

There are two techniques for this process, but both will require this first step. You need to think about what the perfect you looks, acts and feels like. You shouldn't cheat yourself out of the perfect you. You must visualize BIG. This requires you to put some thought into it. The more complete the mental image you start out with, the better results you will have from visualization. This image should contain elements from all of your senses. What do you see, hear, feel, smell and taste?

Questions to help guide the image along:

- What are you wearing? Is it a suit? You must be going to something formal, such as getting an award (which one?). Or are you wearing swimwear? Maybe you are vacationing at the beach. You deserve it after reaching such lofty goals.

- Are you leaner or more muscularly defined? Your exercise plan must be going very well! Are you lifting weights or long-distance running?

- How about your health? You must have cleaned up your diet. How does being healthy feel? Do you have less achy knees and less indigestion or stomach problems? How old are you? Is this two years or more in the future?

- What does it/you smell like? It always smells like chocolate chip cookies for me because I can't think of any unhappy cookie memories.

The most important questions to ask yourself, once you have built this image of the perfect you is:

- How does the perfect me feel?

- What emotions are attached to the perfect me? Am I proud, in love, or have anticipation, joy or calmness?

- Notice that the perfect you has let go of all the emotional baggage of guilt and anxiety. When you have all of the other details figured out, you must attach an emotion to the image. It is this emotion that will help drive you to become this image. Visualization without this attachment is not nearly as useful, as when emotions are the driving force behind it.

In your image, you should have already forgiven yourself and made the improvements you are seeking to forgive yourself. You have accepted who you are and improved it.

With this important first step complete, we can move on to the next steps.

You can use the visualization technique in two different but equally useful ways. Process Visualization and Outcome Visualization are both well-recognized performance enhancing drills.

Process Visualization: It can be thought of as mental practicing. We are going to use our perfect self-image and animate it into performing the tasks we need to do to improve every aspect of our lives, including forgiving ourselves. This versatile form of visualization can be used to see ourselves re-enacting events to forgive and accept or to see yourself already performing needed tasks. If could mean exercising to get into shape or finishing work that we procrastinate on. Let's look at several examples to illustrate what we are looking for.

Using the image of yourself you created above, we are going to explore process visualization and how it can be used for forgiveness. When using it to forgive past events or injustices, you need to picture yourself doing the steps you would require to be forgiven. First, you must see the event that caused the problem, then visualize yourself doing what you wish you had done originally. Allow yourself to feel how good you would have had you done it correctly. The pride, the satisfaction or just the smile it would have given you. Run yourself through all steps you think need to be done for success until you are certain that, given another chance, you would perform the task well. Now feel the reward you have envisioned for task, and then forgive yourself. Going through this process makes it easier to accept your mistake and real-ize that further emotional upset over this event is not a beneficial to you or anyone else. Know that the mental preparation you just did will be how you react next time; you've already trained for it mentally. You are now a bet-ter person and have mastered this lesson. At the end of your visualization, it should feel like you have already reacted the appropriate way at least once before. You have completed the mental drill, and all that is left is to run through the physical motions, should the need arise.

We will next use our mental image to picture ourselves doing something that we feel guilty about. Let's use the example of 'you need to exercise more'. Picture yourself running, with each foot falling in the correct rhythm. Your breath is coming fast but even and steady. The miles/km are vanishing with every step, creating a better you. Your running form is impeccable. Think about how far each leg goes back, how the foot falls and how the push off happens. It is smooth. How does it feel to be running and achieving that goal? You should remember to add in the emotions you are feeling by achieving your goal.

This kind of visualization can elevate your performance to new heights. It is practiced by nearly all Olympic level athletes and in many professional sports. It will help you get off the couch and start moving. You will want to strive to do well. The firm mental image of you performing, convinces you that you can. If you have guilt over your body image or a lack of fitness, this can be a win-win for you. This includes whether you intend to run, bike, swim, lift or do any other fitness training.

Visualization can also be used for other events or tasks. For example, do you want to be a writer and create the next bestselling book? If so, imagine yourself writing the chapters for your book. There you are, with a smile on your face and tapping away on your computer. You've picked out your format of choice. It is now time to start. The outline is done. It is now time to give the world your imagination and ideas. The typing is easier than ever, and the words are flowing out of you as quickly as your typing allows. You are in a calm state. You are in the flow. It is where ideas come from. This dream is in the process of happening for you.

Any task, whether it is work you dread and you procrastinate about or hobbies you love doing, can benefit from this practice. Envision yourself doing it well and finishing the last part of the task to call it a job well done.

Whatever you need to do to forgive yourself for doing or not doing, imagine the near-perfect version of yourself doing it and being great at it. Think through the entire process. If it is too long a process, then think through the parts one segment at a time. As you do this mental practicing drill, you will feel more prepared and motivated to do it in your daily life. Commit yourself to doing the things that you practice. Process Visualization is a way to practice the most difficult challenges in your life; and to commit the willpower to overcome them when the time comes. Professional athletes will tell you that it works and works well!

Outcome Visualization: This is where you imagine that the tasks are already completed, and you are receiving the accolades. The simplest example would be of you crossing the finish line of a race within your goal time. You can also imagine yourself receiving employee of the month or other awards. You would envision the near perfect you on stage or in front of your colleagues, smiling and with the award in your hand.

We use outcome visualization for forgiveness through the visualization of a state of acceptance. We do this because it is one of the major end goals of forgiveness. We want to reach a state of acceptance with who we are and a realistic understanding of our situation. Outcome visualization is very similar to process visualization. We need a very firm mental image as our starting point. We must attach to that image, the feeling of acceptance. This is because in this visualization we have already forgiven ourselves. It is helpful not only to use acceptance in this image but also gratitude. It is gratitude for all those who forgave you and for finding it in yourself to forgive. The end image is us, filled with acceptance and gratitude, lighter and burden-free from guilt and negative self-thought. We are ready and eager for the next challenge.

Choose to be Happy.

Am I jumping ahead here? Doesn't this chapter come later in the book? Yes, and we will go into it in greater detail. However, choosing to be happy is one way to forgive yourself. Negative and positive emotions cannot co-exist in your brain together. It causes too much cognitive dissonance. The emotions of fear and comfort, disgust and love and sorrow and joy conflict with each other. When they do co-exist, it is usually traumatic or turbulent as the emotions struggle within us for dominance. The ability to choose happiness and enforce it, is within our power. It isn't the easiest route to choose until we've done some additional prep work, as outlined in this book.

The mix of emotions can lead you in the wrong direction. It is usually the negative emotions that win the battle for control in our mind, when we do not actively reinforce the positive. The instinctual part of our minds have been programmed that way. Negative emotions, such as fear and anxiety, allowed us to enjoy longer lives, when we were hunted as prey by wolves and lions. That is no longer the situation. That is great news for us now. However, in the past we were trained to focus on the negative. We must build a new mindset in order to overcome this. It takes mental effort, and some of that finite willpower that we have each day.

Just choosing to be happy can work. It will not work for most people. Even if you are one of those individuals who can manage this feat, I recommend reading the rest of the book. There are tools in this book that will greatly reduce the effort required to maintain that happiness. It is also a guide to building happiness as a habit, not a forced state of mind. If you decide to take a forced approach, you can skip to the chapter on choosing happiness for a more detailed guide.

There are some possible pitfalls of willing yourself to be happy as a route to lasting happiness. The purpose of this discussion is not to scare you, but to advise you to be on the lookout for them and to avoid them.

Pitfalls:

There are some possible pitfalls of willing yourself happy as a route to lasting happiness. The purpose of this discussion is not to scare you, but to advise you to be on the lookout for them and to avoid them. As I will discuss in a later chapter, you only have so much willpower in a day. When we are attempting to build a habit, we have to go against some other already established habit. Even if that pattern is sitting on the couch doing nothing, it is still a habit that we have to break while building another one. Whenever we go against those pre-established practices in our life, it requires willpower.

Emotions are also a habit. Letting emotions choose themselves or letting events choose emotions for you, is a habit. It is probably one that you have had your entire adult life. Choosing happiness requires a full day of commitment and effort that can be overwhelming and result in failure. Your willpower is finite. Choosing to be happy can leave you in the turbulent state discussed above. You will be pitting happiness against negative emotions, if you have not forgiven yourself first.

Why should I do it?

"Forgiveness is a gift to yourself. It frees you from the past (including past experiences and past relationships). It allows you to live in the present time. When you forgive yourself and forgive others, you are indeed free."
-Louise Hay

When we carry negative emotions, guilt and remorse around with us on a daily basis it affects how we view and react to the world around us. Learning to forgive ourselves allows us to alter how we see events around us and handle them in a much more positive way.

Example:

A big burly man bumps into you on the sidewalk. Is your first reaction negative? Is it the "Hey watch it buddy!" response? I would like you to think about this reaction for a moment. Yes, someone pushing you might warrant that reaction. However, someone stumbling does not. Big and burly or not, he didn't purposely cause you harm or think to himself how cool he looked doing it. What if that big hairy and burly guy was replaced by someone who is very attractive or a child? We have pre-existing positive feelings toward both of them. As a result, our reaction to being stumbled into, will more likely be "Hey, are you OK?" Our preexisting negative feelings toward the big guy tainted our response. It also increased the likelihood of the guy reacting aggressively towards you and giving you a thumping. Your negative image of him created a negative response. As a result, you got a negative kick in the pants.

This may seem like a silly example, but it is very true to how most people would handle it. It's the same thing that happens when we hold on to negative thoughts of ourselves. When we stumble we say, "Damn I'm such a klutz!" instead of "Whoa, I better be careful!" Then we spend some time being grumpy and kicking ourselves about it, instead of moving on. We need to replace our feelings of inadequacy with the understanding that we are growing, improving, and that making mistakes is how we learn to become better.

Negative emotions focus us on the negative events to a point where that becomes all we see. Once that happens it creates even more problems. We create from those perceptions a world were nearly all things are identified by their negative aspects. It leaches happiness and the sense of well-being from you making happiness something that only happens on rare occasions. We need to use forgiveness of ourselves and others to release these toxic negative emotions and perceptions. Once built into a habit this tool will build a foundation for the happiness we are going to build into our daily lives.

Why does Visualization work?

There are two theories about why the pure statement and the visualization techniques are useful in dealing with forgiving yourself. They come from lessons in Cognitive Behavior Therapy and the Principle of Cognitive Consistency. Both have information as to why these simple techniques are useful. Let's start with Cognitive Behavior therapy.

CBT is short-term (as in it works quickly) psychotherapy. It is a goal-oriented treatment that takes a hands-on, practical approach to solving a wide variety of problems. It attempts to change behavior or thought

patterns that are the cause of people's suffering. Therefore, it changes the way that they feel. CBT in its simplest form addresses the circular nature of our thoughts,
emotions and behaviors.

THOUGHTS
What we THINK affects
how we act and feel

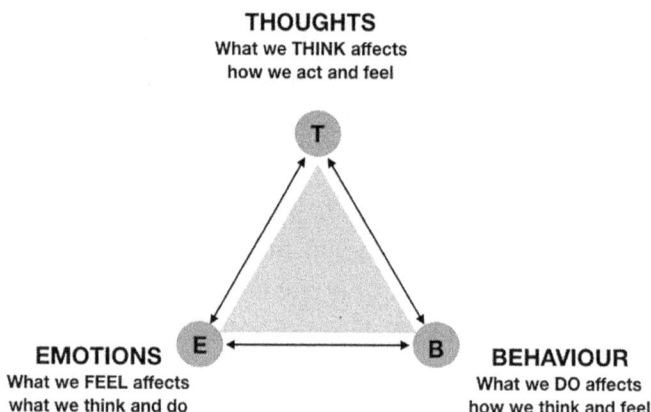

EMOTIONS
What we FEEL affects
what we think and do

BEHAVIOUR
What we DO affects
how we think and feel

Dr. Aaron Beck, the inventor of CBT, saw the link
between thoughts and emotions. He understood how
important it was. He also invented a term called "auto-
matic thoughts". These are emotion-filled thoughts that
occasionally pop up in your head. Dr. Beck discovered
that people were not recognizing these thoughts as having such a negative impact, especially when they came
with strong emotions attached. They could, however,
be taught to identify and report them. If someone was
upset, the thoughts were usually negative, unrealistic and
not all helpful to the individual. Beck found that learning to identify these nonproductive thoughts was a major
step in overcoming potentially serious difficulties.

Dr. Beck named it cognitive therapy because of the

importance it places on thinking. It is now called cognitive-behavioral therapy (CBT) because treatment uses behavioral techniques along with the identification of negative thoughts and emotions.

Stating you deserve forgiveness (behavior) triggers negative thoughts (thought) about specific events that are creating the emotional guilt (emotions) that is preventing you from feeling happy. With the thought now identified and addressed you have changed the emotion you connected to it and that in turn changes your behavior and emotional reaction to it. This then changes your thought patterns and the cycle repeats. I am sure that every psychotherapist on the planet just frowned a little about this over-simplification of a complicated brain function. Like all things in our psyche, it is more complicated. However, we will leave it simple for our purposes. We are going to discuss CBT in every chapter. It is very effective treatment for depression, PTSD, anxiety, OCD and anger problems. These same basic principles can help you to achieve lasting happiness.

"A vision is not just a picture of what could be; it is an appeal to our better selves, a call to become something more."
-Rosabeth Moss Kanter

Cognitive Consistency Theory and Cognitive Dissonance Theory are similar theories about why we react in certain ways and we can use that knowledge to our advantage. Just recognizing it is a great way to prevent ourselves from quitting or falling back into destructive habits. They both refer to a situation involving conflicting attitudes, beliefs or behaviors. When our actions beliefs or emotions are in conflict with each other, it produces a feeling of discomfort that prompts us to change whichever attitude, belief or behavior is out of character. Our mind does this in order to reduce the discomfort and to restore perceived consistency. Both of these theories state that the mind seeks a consistent state at all times. The discomfort between beliefs and our behaviors and attitudes will drive change in one or all three to achieve the comfort of balance. It will do so with or without your permission. It is usually not a conscious decision as to which of these aspects change. That is a change we need to make because it can be. When we visualize ourselves beyond the guilt having already changed our behavior to be consistent with the visualization, it creates this dissonance. When in your visualization you see yourself better, your mind has a choice. It can give up on the visualization or improve to match the thoughts and beliefs. You are going to insure it isn't the visualization that the mind gives up on by daily practice. You will then naturally strive to balance the inconsistency between the guilty undeserving vision of yourself and this new near-perfect version of yourself. It is not likely that this process will work the instantly. You will have to keep reasserting the near perfect you visualization to maintain the tension between it and the former you. We all love the easy path and so does our brain. It will try to convince you to stop visualizing, because it is not working. This will be the easiest route to achieve balance, but it will result with you right back where you started. If you keep at it, it will work. Here is a typical example that is used to help clarify what I am trying to explain.

Most people who smoke, know that smoking is bad for their health. However, they still choose to participate in the act (behavior) of smoking. They experience cognitive dissonance. Why do so many smokers never give up smoking, even if they are experiencing discomfort from cognitive dissonance? To recreate the balance, they intentionally question and disbelieve one of the aspects. Due to the nature of addiction, it is often far easier to disbelieve the health risk, because it is the quickest way to dissolve the imbalance. We tend to hear these types of statements from them: "My Dad smoked his whole life and lived to 80," and "I'm only taking off the years I would be old and frail," "I don't smoke enough to cause a health problem," and my favorite "You have to die of something." Those are all beliefs and statements the mind grabs onto, in order to level the inconsistency between the wanting to be healthy (thought) and smoking (behavior.)

One of the reasons we inject so much detail into the visualization is to foster the discomfort and to better emphasize the difference. Your visualization needs to seem so real that the thought of not striving to be your near perfect self, would leave you feeling uncomfortable. Instead of allowing yourself to balance the inconsistency by falsely assuming you are not that person or quitting, you are going to visualize it again. Success in this task means you are going to keep visualizing it until to not act like the near perfect you is uncomfortable. If you put enough certainty into the vision, it can be a quick process. Visualize-Believe-then Act. The acting part will only be hard the first few times. You will then become that person. It will be harder to not jump into action because it would be inconsistent with your beliefs and attitudes about yourself. It is because you are awesome!

My Story:

My struggle with self-forgiveness didn't surface for me, until about six months after returning from Iraq the first time. We were a unit already prepping to deploy again. I loved being with my children. But the looming redeployment tainted much of the interactions. I felt so guilty for needing to leave them again. My marriage was also a wreck. For that reason alone, I started looking forward to the away time. It wasn't like I was spending much of my "home" time at home anyway with all the pre-deployment training and schools. The feeling of joy about escape fostered even more by guilt about the absences from my children.

We had unit training events that took us away periodically for a week or two at a time and then a month. I then needed to attend some specialized training that took me away for seven weeks. Between all that intrusive thoughts from the previous deployment of shots fired and unfired, made it feel like there no time in my life for happiness. There were regrets and feelings of shame for my non-presence style of fathering. I had guilt and remorse from several of my engagements in Iraq. I felt like a failure in my marriage. These were major events, and they convinced me that I was not a good man or father.

Once I started down that path, the negative emotional thoughts started increasing at a rapid rate. It sapped energy from me and soon I also had poor physical conditioning producing 'unfit to serve' fears. I manifested an aversion to the thought of engaging again which caused further guilt and worry that when the time came, I would not be able to do my job. This continued for about three months. In the end, I felt crippled and not worthy of the army or my family's efforts. I had so effectively beaten myself down with imaginary ailments and self-destructive thoughts, that I felt worthless. As an aviator, I felt it wasn't possible to get help that wasn't both embarrassing and career ending.

While visiting my parents, my mom remarked that she didn't think she had seen my old happy self for many years. I hadn't even realized it was showing at all, not to mention that it had been showing for years.

That statement from my mother wore at me my entire visit. It became what my mind drifted to, when not playing with my amazing children or talking to my parents. I thought back to what my father had taught me many years ago. I picked up books and read articles in secret, looking for a way through it. I reflected on my guilt and worries. I found that most of what was bogging me down was not even real. They were assumptions from real events in my life that were blown out of proportion sometimes to extreme extents. They often had no basis in my real life. These negative thoughts were reproducing themselves and I hadn't noticed it. They had taken the things I should have been addressing and buried them so deeply that I couldn't recognize the root problem without digging through it. I started saying it aloud.

"I deserve forgiveness for all the things I have been holding on to. I forgive me."

"Oh no, you don't! Guilty unhappiness is the new consistency in this joint! Don't forget about...."

So, I said it again over and over again. It didn't take long. Negative thoughts are not as hard to kick as you think they are. It left me with a few things that I needed to forgive myself for, in order to feel happy again. Once I was able to get through the unreal and unrealistic, I wasn't left with many major things to forgive myself for. It took me about three weeks. I shed secluded tears, eliminated unrealistic standards and it felt like I had set down the weight of the moon. After that, I looked at myself differently. I saw the real me and the real situation that I had gotten myself into. I accepted my role in it and made changes so that I could return to a path for success. The feeling of relief from it all was intoxicating. It was a new life and a chance to be the man that I knew I could be. I had stopped seeing myself as dominated by my flaws and then forgave myself because I was never meant to be perfect.

CHAPTER THREE
─────────────

Searching for the Positive

"Once you replace negative thoughts with positive ones,
you'll start having positive results."
- Willie Nelson

IT'S TIME TO take a spin on the positive side or spin
things into a positive. Both are equally true!

The Concept:

Positive thoughts attract positive attitudes and the
right people into your life. There is a positive side to
all the negativity in your life. It can be as simple as an
opportunity to laugh or it can be a lesson you needed to
learn. You must look for, find and focus on those positive aspects before they can become beneficial. Once you
start doing so, you will have a hard time not seeing the
positive, even in the most difficult situations.

What do I have to do?

You must start looking for the positive in everything. It is there, I promise. Even in the worse situation, there will be a glimmer of positivity although it may not be apparent to begin with. It may take days or even weeks to recognize the lesson, but a positive ALWAYS comes from a negative.

We are going to make simple changes in the way you view the world and start hunting the positives. Your work whether it is in an office or in your own home is the perfect place to start. We generally spend more hours at work than we do with anywhere else. Imagine not dreading going in, wouldn't it be more productive for you and those around you, if you were happy and positive? Even if you dislike your current job there are strong reasons to start hunting the good aspects. Trying to find those positives will change how you react to every situation, it improves your performance and helps bring happiness to the for front of your day. Maybe you like spending time with your colleagues, or your boss lets you leave ten minutes early every day or the company provides the most amazing coffee. There will be something to brighten up your day.

Another way to find positive things in your day is to learn to ask better questions. Negative questions such as "Why me?" and "Why didn't so and so do it?" often create angry thoughts that are not productive on any level. You must accept how destructive, time-consuming, team destroying and pointless blame is for one and understand how to ask questions that make improvement for

another. Reframing your thoughts and asking productive questions will make more difference in the quality of
your day than most people are willing to believe prior to
trying it themselves.

How do you do it?

Positive Spin doctor to the rescue!

The concept of finding positives in everything,
including the bad times, may seem like an arduous task
to many people. Training your brain to acknowledge
positives can have a ripple effect through all aspects of
your life. I know that finding the positive in events can
be difficult, especially when we are feeling overwhelmed
by everything that is happening to us. It is worth the
effort. Once you head down this path you will notice an
improvement in your mood in no time.

Seeking out the positives is a fun and liberating experience. You should start big and seek positivity in all
of the difficult things in your life. Everything from the
last-minute work assignment that was due yesterday to
stubbing your toe in the morning. Ask yourself, "What
possible good can come from a stubbed toe?" All that
hopping around got your blood pumping, right? Did
you blurt out an expletive(s)? Stress relief! Was there
someone at home that checked on you and asked if you
were OK? That is loving attention. Did you both laugh
about it? It is bonding and healing laughter. I know that
this might sound odd to some people. Unless you try it,
you'll never experience the wonderful insights you'll get

from this easy and valuable exercise. You might feel silly doing it at first. Nevertheless, I urge you to try it. I know that you'll be pleasantly surprised.

Finding positive in situations isn't the same as saying there that there are no negatives. Stubbing a toe hurts like crazy and last-minute work assignments are annoying and stressful. You shouldn't devalue the bad. Doing so reduces the triumph you feel for overcoming and isn't realistic. Focus instead on the positive you will get from that challenge. Although it will take some practice, it will be worth it.

When I am having problems identifying the positive in a situation, I ask myself this series of questions:

• What does the ideal result look like in this situation? It might be a ridiculous answer. It is usually a great place to start putting the problem into perspective. It also allows you to see possible positive elements during the fixing process.

• Who am I going to need to work with to fix this? It can be a real pleasure working through a problem with other people. You might get the pleasure of meeting a new person during this process. That is a bonus.

• When is the due date for this fix? You might have some time, which is always something to be grateful for, but also you might get to take a break on something tedious to make the fix happen.

- Why was I the one selected to find the solution? It is a very good complement to be singled out as a problem fixer. The 'why' might be because you are the brightest, best qualified or you are the easiest to work with. Any way you look at it, it is a compliment and an opportunity to show people your new positive attitude.

We are so used to focusing on the bad in our lives that it can be a big shift to search for the good in everything which happens to us. Once you get started, you are going to be addicted to the positive side. It's an entirely new mindset that you will become accustomed to. You should start now. Don't wait for bad things to happen. You should practice before things get out of hand.

We aren't trying to put a false face on the bad. We are trying to shift focus to the positive outcomes and benefits from the bad. Hurricane Katrina, for example, was a devastating event in our country. It also uncovered nationwide corruption, helped to rebuild a failing city and improved racial tensions in the area. All of these things occurred soon after the devastating events. It was not necessary to wait years in order to see positive from such a tragedy.

Another example is dieting. Occasionally going off a diet can reinvigorate exercise programs and the diet itself. Getting into a fender bender lets you meet new people and appreciate the advances in car safety. There is ALWAYS good in our lives. It isn't always easy to see it initially. However, once you start looking, you will find it. After a while, it will dominate your perception of all events. Even if you can't immediately find something positive, try to find some humor in it. A laugh is a positive event.

Change Your Reputation

Your reputation is based on everything from your appearance to your actions. Once established, it can be difficult to change. In the Army, people were moved to different units or positions because of bad reputations. Even then retraining and a job change can't always help a person with a bad reputation. As the old saying goes: It takes years to build a reputation and seconds to destroy it.

People with bad attitudes at work and who are constantly expressing negative views of themselves or others, don't usually fit in anywhere. Since these two negative attributes are often linked, it is necessary to address them both.

Let me start by saying that you are super great! There is no question in my mind about it. I know this because of the type of person who picks up a book like this. The desire for self-improvement is far more valuable than all the formal training, seminars, gym workouts or CrossFit that you could do. We will work on self-image throughout the book. If you already feel like you are great, you're right. There is no limit to the amount of greatness in you. Even if your reputation isn't negative, there is still room for some improvement. We want it to become overwhelmingly positive. This should not be confused with being bubbly. That is not what I am talking about, even though it is often the first image that comes to mind. It also doesn't mean that you need to start saying 'yes' more, although that was one of my positive results.

You need to be the person in the office who people know will react well to all news. Your reputation will be helped by seeing the positive in events and be further enhanced by avoiding the blame game. You need to build a reputation as a positive person. Once you have established this, you will be pleasantly surprised by the change in the way people interact with you. People love to be around positive people, that includes your boss and your love interest. It is much easier and enjoyable to work with and around people with good attitudes. You will be one of those people who others are drawn to. As a result, work will become more fun. It will be a fantastic transformation for you and provide smile fuel for months afterwards.

As you become more positive those around you will also, they won't be able to help themselves. In addition to always recognizing the positive aspects to situations, you will accomplish more during your day and naturally ask better questions.

Congratulations!!! You have had your last publicly bad day! From now on when asked "How are you?" you need to say loud and proud that you are "Super Great!" or "Fantabulous!" "Amazing!" It is even better to make up your own super positive responses. I have told people that my day is super great so many times with enthusiasm, people actually get excited about asking me how

I am doing! I know this seems overly simple and even goofy. It works and works well! You want to tell anyone that asks how absolutely incredible things are for you right now. Someone cared enough to ask how your day was. It is a great perk to give them a boost in return. Your smile alone will do it. Don't limit yourself to just that. You need to give them your best answer! If I seem to be fanatical about this practice, it' is because I am! It has been a life-changing concept for me. I am super great, and you can be too.

I no longer wait for others to ask me about my day. I ask them first and listen to their answer. Most people around me now say "Super Great!" or "Excellent". This habit is contagious. It is with good reason. When they ask, in return I blast positivity at them with my reply. Many of the people you encounter will ask why you are doing so well. This is great. Even if your day isn't going as well as usual, you can always find a positive spin lesson to tell them. For example: "Work/management have provided me with some challenges today. I am crushing them!!" "Tough days make the regular ones seem like a vacation." There are stacks of positive spins for rough days, which you should use.

How do you know if you already have a negative reputation? A lot of people in the organizations I have worked with have had no idea they had a negative reputation. It never even occurred to them. Some good clues that you have a bad reputation are: People won't ask you how your day is. That is a good indication that your reputation needs work. People also avoid negative people unless they too are negative. Look to the people around you, do they complain or gripe about others, the work, the pay, the parking, or every other imaginable thing? Many of us do that a little but do they ever say anything that isn't disparaging? If they do it is likely your reputation is as bad as theirs is if not worse.

How can you change your negative reputation to a positive one?

- You should start by asking how other people's days are going. If they don't ask you in return, don't be disappointed. They will eventually come around as word starts going through the office that you are a new person. You might initially have to go a little overboard in order to build some momentum. The "super great" ritual of smile and reply is usually enough to start changing your reputation. Here are some additional ideas to help invigorate the progress.

- Help someone else in the workplace. We all know a person who is struggling at work. It might even be you. If it is, you will know which person is in the trenches with you. Give them 30 minutes of your time today. I constructed an extra 30 minutes in my schedule by eating lunch in the office and hopping right back to work. Then when your target person gets set back to work after their break ask them. You should tell them exactly what you are up to. "I have made 30 minutes in my schedule to help you with what you are working on. What can I do?" It doesn't matter if the response is as simple as running downstairs to grab more paper for the printer. This could be all that someone needs to help them with their day. By helping other people, you will be truly overwhelmed by the appreciation and positive responses you will receive. We all have our own work as well, what if you're also busy? I have rarely had to help for the full 30 minutes. Most people just like to have something small taken off their to-do list. They will be happy for the help. You need to be cautious with those individuals who will see the new you as a pushover. They might try to dump their workload on you. Being positive and friendly doesn't mean that you can't say no, if you're too busy for something large.

• Dress for the smile. There are dress codes in most businesses. That doesn't mean you can't add your own flare. Take a close look at your work wardrobe. Is there a way that you can add a splash of color and personality to what you are wearing? Most women in the workplace do this far better than men. Nevertheless, there are options for both. An accent of color can make a major difference when it comes to first impressions. A power tie, pocket square or even one colored button can make a difference. There are strict uniform requirements in my workplace. Therefore, I display a chrome and pink pencil, in the spot where a pocket square would go. These little upgrades add a personal touch to what you are wearing. It is great to take pride in your appearance. These little touches can go a long way towards boosting your self-confidence and self-image. If you give someone a chance to compliment you, it can soften them to the idea of your positive reputation.

Better questions.

You also need to learn to ask better questions. Questions like "why me?" have never helped anyone. "Why do I have to...?" "Why is it always my job to?" "Why doesn't so and so ..." "Why is the other department not...?" No one has ever received an answer to those negative questions that they have liked. There are many alternatives to this type of question. Mostly questions like that are used to garner pity from the other person or they could be the start of a self-destructive thought cycle that will suck you in, waste your time and crush your happiness.

"IT'S A TRAP!" If only Admiral Akbar was there to yell it at you, so you know when you have started down that path. Imagine a day like any other, with the boss walking over to you. He has that look again! Something is wrong, and he is going to hand it off to you. On this new path you are walking, where you ask better questions, my first tip is to take a breath. During that breathe you should: smile (always), and throw away the knee-jerk, unhelpful standard question you were about to ask. It is always better to respond than to react. You should prepare to handle it like a pro. It is necessary to avoid the impulse to point a finger, claim it's not your job or any other similar reactions. You are about to own this problem with a smile. When you own the problem, you also own the opportunity that it brings.

When the boss does drop his bad news on you, ask yourself "What can I do right now to improve this?" and "How can I help the team do this better?" They are great questions for nearly all problems. Adapting them to different situations is quick and easy. If possible, do something to improve the issue immediately. It should be done while the boss is still there handing off the problem. Again smile, someone just handed you a great opportunity to change your reputation to that of a positive action taker. It's time to take ownership of it.

One of my favorite books on asking the right question is QBQ! The Question behind the Question: Practicing Personal Accountability at Work and in Life, by John G. Miller. In this excellent book, Miller defined ownership: as:

"A commitment of the head, heart, and hands to fix the problem and never again affix the blame."

Owning the problem makes it easier to approach it with the right attitude. When you start asking "What can I do and where can I do better," you create positive thoughts and feelings. This increases your job satisfaction and gives you an opportunity to be seen as a positive person.

It is important to remember that it is not your job to hunt down who is at fault. Whichever job, duty or area of responsibility the problem came from, is now yours. It has become a common practice in most work places to attribute blame to a person or team. I have even heard that it is still called a 'witch hunt' in upper-level banking.

I took the time to ask if the approach of attributing blame was a positive concept for the company as a whole. Nobody said that they were happy with this style of management. Even when an individual was found to be at fault, it wasn't a satisfying result. They all admit that it significantly increased tension between everyone in the office and resulted in considerable wasted time and effort. It also results in office drama with everyone on edge. They are preparing to defend themselves all the time. To compound the problem, it creates an unhappy workplace, with a culture of bad news and rumors.

During my time in the military, I have worked in these types of negative environments. They are destructive and hamper productivity. I approach problems using this simple method:

- Verify that the problem is what we think it is.

- Find a solution that works now and work the solution.

- Figure out why we had a problem.

- Repair the why answer, so it doesn't happen again.

- It is important to notice that it does not say: find out WHO screwed up. The who isn't important, until you are in charge. Just remember to ask yourself when the last time was that you were happy with the results of the blame game.

How do you stop the blame game from wasting your time? You can just refuse to participate in it, when the blame starts going around. This is a great method to help to remove the negative reputation that you might have. When you are not participating in negativity and gossip, people around you will notice. Demonstrate that amazing smile you've been working on and you will bowl over the crowd. Just diving into finding and working the solution, will be a huge move toward squashing the blame game.

Your momentum toward becoming better will create momentum in others. Your coworkers are initially going to be shocked at the new you. Don't be surprised if after a bit of time, you have help in your effort to work toward the solution. This kind of positive attitude is more infectious than the negative one that you have been clinging on to. You always have the smile on your face. When your coworkers try to drag you into the blame game, remind them that this problem will still be there, regardless of who caused it or why it happened. It is going to be tough at first. Situations that start the blame game in the office are emotional. If you refuse to acknowledge it or to participate in it, the feeling will fade. Work the solution with a smile, and you will do yourself a huge favor. You might even want to thank the person who made the mistake in the first place, just look at all the opportunity they gave you to shine. Bosses and leaders always love a positive solution.

Another useful approach is to accept all of the blame yourself. Once you do that, you can then dive in to find the answers you need. Most of your colleagues will understand that it wasn't your fault. By accepting the blame, you will derail the office witch hunt. I have often used this approach. I can tell you from experience that it works. It works even better when you are the one in charge and responsible for your section. The Army taught me that the leader is to blame, regardless of the outcome. This is a misguided approach. It would take a micromanaging machine to catch every slip up. The leader should accept responsibility in order to continue to make progress. If your boss isn't capable of doing this, do it yourself. Stand up and declare "THIS WHOLE THING IS MY FAULT! WHO CAN HELP ME FIX IT!" Some people might be relieved and step away at this point. Most of them will come around after taking a few minutes to process it. You will gain a reputation as a person of action. It is also unlikely that many people will believe it was your fault in the first place. The blame game disease in the workplace affects both happy people and productivity, so always pass on it.

These are the quickest ways to change your repu-tation. They are just a few of the things that work. Depending on the situation, you may need to try something completely different. As long as you visibly demonstrate positivity, it will help you on your path. Once you start, you will attract a following at your workplace. Your fellow employees crave happiness and job satisfaction. When you begin to show that you have them, your coworkers will want to follow. You should bring them with you on this journey. We need as many supportive smilers as possible in our lives. If you find something that is very effective for shifting a negative reputation to a positive one, share it with those you work with.

Why should I do this?

The reason to seek the positive in life, change your reputation and ask better questions is because it will result in an overwhelming sense of peace and calm. These simple actions can affect your life so dramatically that I considered writing an entire book on just positive spin and seeking the positive. Once your reputation and positive energy are noticed by others, people will change around you. Those who are stuck in the negative might fade away. Others who seek the same self-improvement and satisfaction will get closer to you. They are going to start reinforcing your conviction that you are doing the right thing. It will become apparent how much power is in your actions and thoughts as you become a happier person and drag others along with you.

Your new outlook will dramatically affect your workplace. It will enable you to change the gloomiest workplaces into the meeting halls for super (great) friends. Happiness is the best performance enhancer in the universe. Studies from Harvard University have demonstrated the effect of happiness on the workplace and student performance. The studies (and my personal experience) undeniably confirm how being happy helps you to handle stress and perform better on exams.

Similar studies are now showing that we can also achieve a huge performance boost from our immediate social support structures. I'm not referring to your thousands of Facebook friends. I am referring to those who are immediately around you. They have been craving the same improvements in the workplace. Start the movement in your job towards positive thinking. It will allow you to build a structure where even the hardest tasks are handled easily. As a result, you will get the most job satisfaction you have had in years. Once the people you work with start seeing the positive in you, it will catch on. They will want to know what has caused your dramatic change. Fill them in and invite them on board. Add a few people to your happiness fold and you will have changed your feelings about your work and will start to enjoy your time there. The previously unbearable tasks will be mundane and simple. The support group will be a constant breath of fresh air. Work is better when you don't spend all day telling yourself and those around you that it sucks.

Defeating negative thinking has even more benefits than the amazing boost it will give you at work. In a study published in the Journal of Clinical Psychology about worry and the effects of negative thoughts, it was found that our brains react to these emotions like an actual immediate threat to our safety that must be handled immediately. It triggers our fight or flight response to deal with a situation that does not require it.

Our brains are pre-wired to respond to negative events, behaviors, and words more quickly than to happy ones. When we think positively, our brain assumes that everything is under control and no drastic action is needed. In the first of several studies, people were required to sort things into two categories. Those who claimed to worry 50% of the time or more demonstrated significant problems in their ability to sort objects, as the difficulty of the task increased.

In a follow-up study, they were able to show that the disruption was a result of increased levels of negative thoughts. When you are faced with a complex task, negative thinking hurts your ability to process information quickly and clearly. The negative thoughts and the fight or flight syndrome are taking up too much of your brain's processing power. Thinking negatively about your problems not only doesn't help solve anything, but it also makes it more difficult for you to think of a helpful solution.

Negative thinking can easily become the norm. After thinking negatively for just a week your brain starts to change and key into the negative aspects in your world even more closely than before. This means that negative thinking breeds more negative thinking. It is a process that adversely affects your entire body. People who tend to be stressed and worry, experience devastating health complications. This is because their body is constantly shifting in and out of the fight or flight response. As a result, they experience real stress physical symptoms such as rapid heartbeat, elevated blood pressure and a state of heightened arousal (not the good kind). This stress creates changes in the brain that increase the chance of mental disorders, such as anxiety, depression, ADHD, schizophrenia and mood disorders. When we sit for a minute and think about it, the glass half-empty folks are getting a far worse deal than you thought. Let's snap out of it. A fully empty glass means that I get to stretch my legs, while getting a refill. Once you start always looking for the positive, it will be hard to understand why you would ever have lived any other way.

Another reason why we need to start building a habit of positivity, is due to the lessons that we have learned from cognitive belief therapy. We've previously mentioned that thought, emotions and behaviors are linked in the mind. When we routinely have positive thoughts, our actions will reflect that. It then becomes easier to achieve our objectives, since actions seem less daunting. These thoughts and behaviors then result in a wealth of emotions. Finding the positive in any situation always results in a burst of positive feelings. You get the sense of accomplishment and the jolt positive emotions from the happy side you just discovered. The CBT triangle of simple beliefs linked to emotions and actions is enough to keep us going and enable us to become happier than we previously thought possible.

My story:

In 2011, at Fort Lewis Washington, two OH58D helicopters collided, killing all four aboard, including a long-time friend of mine. The station was already short-handed, and the Army went looking for people to fill the gaps. I volunteered. When I first arrived on station, I spent time being quiet and assessing what I had got myself into. My late friend had been a newly assigned leader in the troop. He had started making improvements that had excited the group of junior aviators. The previous leadership had been worse than toxic. An individual instructor had destroyed cohesion and the sense of a team, which was crucial to operations. He had then removed any chance for them to improve themselves or to be successful in the army. It floored me. I had heard rumors but had no idea of its extent, until I saw it first-hand. When I ask members of the now dysfunctional team how to make the next step in their progression, they all told me that the only path was to leave Fort Lewis and to go somewhere else.

During this time, the Army had halted these moves because the unit was shorthanded and was prepping for deployment. Less than 20% of the group were mission ready. The tone and atmosphere were stoic, depressing and often angry. It was a defeated unit before any battle had taken place. The first time I whipped out my signature "Super Great", I thought that I might get punched in the face. Every question about the unit or the individual's future garnered a negative response. The soldiers didn't feel like they were ever going to be ready for the upcoming deployment. The unit was "the worst in the Army" according to all those I asked. The Maintainers wanted to pull the pilots into an alley for a fistfight rather than render a salute.

I wish I could say that I am exaggerating. However, it really was that bad. People were blaming each other for everything. The blame game took up a large portion of the day. I started by getting some expert advice from my father. After that I stopped observing and dove in.

At this point, I was still too junior for a lead instructor job. However, the office was empty and the more senior instructor in the troop was having other issues. Therefore, with a little support from the troop commander, we started making adjustments. We did everything we could think of from rearranging offices and having BBQs. We arranged in-depth restructuring of training and reprioritized flights. I even started baking birthday cakes for maintainers and forcing everyone to sing. The first one wasn't even a real birthday. I made it up.

We stayed positive. I super great'ed and Fantabulous'ed every day. There was so much desire to be super, that great people clung to it. Everyone in the troop was so hungry for the improvement that it took little time to start seeing the difference. We ate cake and grew together. I wasn't alone while this was happening. We were getting new senior guys in. They joined the crew and started helping the cause. It was an incredible change in the unit. I didn't do it alone, but I know I played my part in it well. We saw fewer people off sick, fewer injuries, people staying later to help the others and study groups popped up everywhere. The first time we progressed a pilot to the next level, the negative walls shattered. They knew that soldiers could make it in this unit.

People enjoyed the job more than ever. The major change was in their attitudes. Things were not doom and gloom any more. They were uplifting and encouraging. They saw the positive in their work and effort and it changed them to positive people. This new attitude made them work harder. We saw the "worst unit in the Army" turn into a combat ready team, with smiles. I will never forget it. The power of positivity changed the soldiers' lives. It also changed mine.

Several months into the changes, the three most experienced and senior pilots stopped me in the parking lot. They congratulated me and marched me into my commander, where I introduced myself as his new Senior Pilot. In my eyes, I was still too junior for the position. There was even a more senior instructor in the unit, but it didn't matter to them. I got the job, and it was the best one I had in my 21 years of service. I was more than super great!

CHAPTER FOUR

Recognize and Reward

The Concept:

WE MUST RECOGNIZE our value and strengths. This requires us to pick out the things we do well and celebrate them. It also allows us to see and internalize our contributions to our work and team.

What do I need to do?

Redefine what exactly a reward is for you. It can't be chocolate cake all the time! We will need to figure out other ways to reward ourselves.

Recognize small victories are achievements and celebrate them. We are used to celebrating more significant victories and we should continue to do so, but the little ones also need their moments to shine. Let's give it to them!

Commit to review your performance for three minutes after work every day. Jot down a small note for yourself. Post-gaming your day should be mostly posi-tives and no more than two negatives.

How do I do it?

What should be a reward:

When you say reward, you immediately think of grand ideas. I imagine unlikely heroes, collecting piles of riches for deeds they accomplished, saving distressed damsels and defeating evil tycoons. Thankfully, the world doesn't have a lot of need for these services. My next go to is chocolate cake. I love it. It is moist and delicious and a great treat on any occasion. If I could afford the calories I would eat it all the time. Food and snacks do make a good occasional reward but be careful not to overdo it. The calories matter to some people, me included, and can lead to bad habits and large hips. Don't exclude cake and candies as a rare treat but only for special celebrations.

There is a huge list of things that I use to treat myself with. I am a reading machine. I read mostly self-help, journals and studies. I also like science fiction and fan-tasy. I love to read, and I enjoy audiobooks even more. My reward is the pleasure of reading science fiction and fantasy novels. The trashier the book, the better it is. You should look at activities that bring you pleasure or joy. Do you like Moto GP racing? You can reward your-self right at your desk with allotting specific amount of time to watch the highlights on the internet.

It is necessary to decide on a time limit for these types

of rewards before starting. I get wrapped up in a book or the million hours of cat videos online just as quickly as the next guy. Set a limit and stick to it. There should be no reason for your boss to think that you are slacking off when used in this manner. The types of rewards that involve enjoying your favorite pastime, can be thought of as "Recharge style" rewards. This where we take a few minutes away from work to refresh the mind, mood and sometimes the body.

I have become a huge fan of walking to recharge my batteries. This doesn't mean that you have to go outside. Just walking to a different department and saying 'hi' to someone is fine. You can climb the stairs to use a bathroom on a different floor, or head to the corner shop for a cold drink. The getting up and moving around refreshes me far better than the cat videos, and it doesn't take any more time. The "Recharge" style of reward is a set amount of time for yourself not doing your normal work duties. It can include videos, saying 'hi' to the IT guy in person, a walk, a refill, or a few minutes to meditate (of which I am an enormous fan).

Another category of reward for me is the "Treat." Due to the way that I was brought up, I immediately think chocolate cake. This is the category where cake belongs, but it doesn't always have to be cake. Any smaller food treat works well. It could be a few gummy bears or strawberries. When I am watching what I eat, I will have carrots, radishes or bell peppers. You don't have to be too indulgent with the food treats. The act of grabbing a snack is a reward. I often don't think about stopping and grabbing lunch once I get absorbed in a project. Therefore, the food treat is a common one for me. You need to think of several things that you will enjoy doing as a reward for yourself. If you are already stopping every 45 minutes for a carrot break, then think of it as a reward. Say "If I can get 45 minutes of consistent work done, then I will grab my carrots." Just changing how you view that habitual carrot, benefits your mindset and helps you to identify progress.

Another type of reward that I like to use is the "Exclamation!" I will admit that this can stir up those around you. A positive outburst can often become infectious in a room. When that happens, you have done something truly great. You are spreading a little joy, even if it was unintentional. I use "Hell YEAH!" a lot and just to be different "HAZZAA!" It sounds a little corny, but it works. It creates a little spark of joy every time that I do it. I only use it when I have reached a minor goal. It feels good and lets the team that know progress is being made. Exclamations do not have to be out loud. If you work where it isn't appropriate, like, for example, a surgical nurse, bomb technician or a maternity ward, then exclamations can be entirely internal. The mental high fives, arms pumping or a bit of chair dancing work just as well.

We now have a list of possible ways to celebrate rewards. The next step is to look at what is reward worthy. You might be surprised it is such a long list. The list is so long that we will just look at the more common types. However, don't let it stop you from adding your own reward for the work that you do.

When should you reward:

A "Time Based" approach for when to reward yourself works especially well for projects that are hard to get motivated about. They also work well for tedious tasks or things that require long undistracted attention. In my case, this could include projects such as building a slide presentation or the hours I spend working with Excel. They can be some of the most important things that you do in your day, but still not very exciting.

Choose a length of time you would like to focus on one task. Make sure it is uninterrupted time as much as possible. Let's say you decide to focus on your task between 9 a.m. and 10:30 a.m. As you work you might clock watch, but once you get into the swing of things, you will be surprised at how quickly the time goes. As 10:30 a.m. approaches, you might even notice that your work pace increases. It's like a mini-deadline pushing you to achieve more than you normally would. Once you see the clock reading 10:30 a.m., stop you deserve your reward. Take it with a smile!

The "Event-Based" approach assumes that you already know the goals or directions for your project. Your goals could be: "Sign up 35 people," "Get 25 reports done," or "Bathe all the children,". These are things that happen daily or for special projects. This type of goal works great when you have things to complete or a set number of things to do. It motivates you through the process when you have established when and how you will treat yourself. I find that I get my tasks done much faster when I work this way with clear stopping points and something to look forward to. I like that feeling of accomplishment I get when I do this.

The "Landmark-Based" events are usually and rare. Landmarks are generally the big projects coming to an end or switching phases. You can usually see these coming pretty far out so plan something special for them. They are a cause for celebration with everyone working on the project. It may only be you if you work solo. When it is more than you, try to include everyone working on it in your celebration. This helps build the team and creates positive enthusiasm for the group. Bring them along for a celebration out or slice them a piece of the cake as a reward for your collective accomplishment.

The "Breakthrough based" approach is even harder to predict. Therefore, you are going to have to be a bit more spontaneous with how you celebrate and recognize them. Breakthroughs are huge and are often a reward in themselves. You should celebrate breakthroughs in a group whenever possible. Even people working for themselves have loved ones to celebrate their breakthroughs with. My first breakthrough while writing this book was realizing that I would never get it done if I continued editing along the way. Once I stopped doing that, it was a true breakthrough for me. I celebrated by calling my father.

We celebrated with exclamations and laughter together. I followed it with a writing binge!

Celebrating isn't just for those work-based accomplishments. This isn't a finding happiness at work book. This book is about living life happy, so we have to look for these gems and celebrate them. As we begin looking for the positive in our lives, like in the previous chapter, you will find plenty of events that require no spin to see as positive or happy situations. Simple acts of kindness, both given and received, are worthy of celebration. I often do something for someone AS a celebration, just because it feels good.

Many of us have trained ourselves to tune out the small affirming events that happen to us every day. Our world is obsessed with bad news and horrible predictions. It draws us in, and soon we see little else. It has become so oppressive that people have started striking out as crusaders against the gloom. Paying for the coffee of the person behind you isn't a new thing. People have done that for years. Thankfully now with social media and instant messaging people are celebrating those little perks and sharing it with a larger group than ever.

Strangers are putting money in parking meters just as they run out, tolls are being paid, popcorn is bought for the guy behind you at the theatre and someone is cleaning the coffee pot at work. People "Paying it forward" is always a good thing to see on social media, regardless of the intentions behind it. All these seemingly small things deserve a WHOOP or a full smile. We should be on the lookout and celebrate even the small uplifting moments. This could include: waking and feeling rested, receiving a compliment or an uplifting text, someone singing in the car a lane over, or someone dancing through their gym workout. They're not the events that we should break out the champagne for, but you should still give them a moment of recognition. Smile, laugh, sing along, or just get the cake out.

Big celebrations for small events can be a laugh and fun for all! You need to look for things to celebrate. If you can't find one (which I find unlikely) by noon, then it's time to make a reason for celebrating. Buy a coffee for the guy behind you. Making someone else's day is an awesome reason to feel great and celebrate. Throw out a deserved compliment and celebrate Beth's new red shoes because they look damn good! When we search for the happy celebrations in our life, we are going to start finding them all the time. The best part is to bring as many to the party as you can. Build those up around you who want to chair dance, have cake, dance to the rhythm and celebrate the good things in life.

After each day at the office, I used to find my mind repeatedly wandering back to the day's achievements and mistakes. It is part of our nature to seek self-improvement. Questions such as "Why didn't I do this right?" or "Why did I let this happen?" can drag us back to our workplace to review the same errors over and over again. It is like they are set on repeat. It's mostly nonproductive and distracts us from living in the moment. It can leave your significant others feeling unimportant and your friends feeling like you are disinterested in them. This replaying is almost exclusively around the negative parts of the day. It can even spill over into analyzing conversations that you had, where you either beat yourself up over what you said or twist something so that you end up in a negative spin. I always first recommend meditation for cycles like this. In fact, I recommend it for everyone, even those who are not struggling. Meditation is an excellent way to train your mind against destructive intrusive thoughts. There are many fantastic resources and people willing to teach meditation. It deserves more attention than I can give it here. I like "The Relaxation and Stress Reduction Workbook" by M. Mckay, M. Davis, E. Elizabeth and P. Fanning. It is in its 6th edition. Its many fantastic tools contain some of the best descriptions of simple nonreligious/spiritual meditation I have found anywhere.

Another fantastic resource is "*Mindfulness in Plain English*" by Bhante Gunaratana. A quick, easy guide to meditation can be found on youtube.com by searching for Improvement Pill's-"How to Meditate for Beginner-A Definitive Guide". These are all excellent gateways into the single healthiest thing you can do in just 15 minutes. Although I won't be going into any more meditation instructions here, I have another task that can help you to reduce the amount of time your mind spends dragging you back to work. It will also be quicker to perform and start working nearly immediately. After you have finished your last to-do thing at work, start a three-minute timer and critique your day. Try and think of the things you've done well and the things you need to improve. Once you reach a max of two needs improvements switch your focus to the things you've done well. Write them down on a post-it while thinking of them or after the three minutes are up. Just list the event and not the steps to improve. Once it is complete, put it somewhere you will see it the first thing in the morning. It will be there the next day at the exact right place and time for you to take action. When you get into work smiling and full of uncontained joy the next morning, look at your note and think about how to improve the things you listed. You should also review the things you did well. After doing this exercise for a week, you will start to see a pattern of things that you do well. I love this exercise for several reasons. It limits my time for self-critique and prevents me from plunging into a self-doubt hole. It also allows me to address the things that I can do better. This is an amazing way to spend the first few minutes of any day. It is a little self-improvement and patting on the back.

What are your personal strengths? The answer to this question is important to firmly identify and write down. I shine in stressful situations and do some of my best work under pressure. I am a skilled people person and have no problem getting along with anyone. I also am a top tier instructor. I am a creative mediator. When we handle work tasks using our strengths, we are fifteen times more likely to call our day happy. Studies on workday happiness suggest that it doesn't even matter what happened in the rest of our day as long as we used the skills we consider our strengths to accomplish one thing. There are several surveys and tools available to help identify your strengths. www.16personalities.com is good at pointing you in the right direction if you are not sure of what your areas of strength are. My favorite for the identification of strengths you should be using at work is www.viacharacter.org. My number one personality trait is creativity. I find that my days are far better when I get to use that skill at work or with my friends. Once you know what your strengths are, try and implement them into your job at least a few times a week.

Why should you do it?

When we search for things to celebrate in our day, it highlights our accomplishments building a sense of value to our work. Rewarding focuses on building positive emotions and feelings, especially about ourselves. It's also about positive behaviors, depending on what the reward you intend to give yourself. Those positive emotions and behaviors build self-confidence and a sense of value to our work, it's like a storehouse of positive emotions inside of you that you can fall back on. During my military career, it was referred to as resiliency. When we have all these positives to fall back on during hard times, they just don't hit us as hard. The rewarding process not only emphasizes these emotional treasures, but also ties them to the things you will easily remember.

When we have catastrophic events in our lives, this positive bank of emotions lets us bounce back much quicker. There are two main reasons that this storehouse is so effective when the chips are down.

In order to build a positive emotional bank account, we have to learn to pick the positives out of our days. Just like putting money in an account, we have to identify where the money is coming from and then deposit it. Fortunately, all we have to do is clearly identify them in this case and they get automatically deposited into our reserves. "I had a great day," is awesome isn't as good as "I had a great day because Bob bought me a coffee." It's the difference between depositing a "some money" versus a hundred dollars in your bank. By now I am sure you realize that the reward itself is only a small boost to what we are striving for. It is the habit of seeing your own value and putting yourself in a positive light. Rewarding yourself keeps you searching for the good in your life and the good that you are doing. The reward itself helps you to remember the positive in the world around you.

Your emotions cause physiological changes in your body by programming every cell. This excerpt from "How Your Thoughts Program Your Cells" from Jordan Lejuwaan founder of HighExistence.com describes the science beautifully.

> "There are thousands upon thousands of receptors on each cell in our body. Each receptor is specific to one peptide, or protein. When we have feelings of anger, sadness, guilt, excitement, happiness or

nervousness, each separate emotion releases its own flurry of neuropeptides. Those peptides surge through the body and connect with those receptors which change the structure of each cell as a whole. Where this gets interesting is when the cells actually divide. If a cell has been exposed to a certain peptide more than others, the new cell that is produced through its division will have more of the receptor that matches with that specific peptide. Likewise, the cell will also have less receptors for peptides that its mother/sister cell was not exposed to as often."

What Lejuwaan is saying is that whatever emotion we experience the most, our cells tune themselves to receive. The next generation of cells will be physically set up to receive that feeling and will be less able to receive another type of emotion. For instance, if you are happy most of the time, the next generation of cells produced in your body will have more receptors for the peptide that causes you to feel happy and less for another emotion like anger or sadness. Let that sink in for just a moment... Happiness physically changes the structure of the cells in your body. The first noticeable difference is that you will be more receptive to being happy.

If that wasn't a huge surprise to you, I welcome you to my next revelation, my fellow nerdy friend! It's amazing science but it gets even stranger and, if possible, even more incredible. Your thoughts and emotions determine which genes are active in your body. The field of Epigenetics has definitively proven the mind-body connection. You aren't getting a different genetic makeup with that winning smile. You are just activating different genes sets within your preexisting strands.

Epigenetics shows that your perceptions and thoughts control your biology. By changing your thoughts to be more positive, it can alter which sections of your DNA will be used when producing the next generation of cells. This can have a major impact on your health for many years to come.

In their fabulous book "Connected: The Surprising Power of Our Social Networks and How They Shape Our Lives -- How Your Friends' Friends' Friends Affect Everything You Feel, Think, and Do" by Nicholas A. Christakis and James H. Fowler looked into our social networks and the contagions of attitudes and beliefs that spread in them. In one of my favorite parts of the book, we learn how your attitudes and conduct spread three people deep. Your small good deed causes another and another through three people. You are affecting or infecting more and more down that line, long after any either negative or positive act. They estimate that you could easily touch 1,000 people a day. That is 1,000 people who get perked up by one heartfelt compliment, or 1,000 poor waitresses yelled at, because you gave a guy the finger in traffic. I know which chain I would rather start. That is why I go out of my way to compliment, smile, and have positive interactions with everyone. The impact you have positive or negative is far reaching.

Another reason why you should be rewarding and identifying the good stuff is the Cognitive Behavior Therapy triangle again. Rewarding is an emotional win every time for those involved. It also prompts positive responses, since rewards are generally positive behavior that create even more positive emotions. We are getting a double whammy on the triangle of CBT happiness for rewarding ourselves. There is one in emotions and one in behaviors. It is also a great illustration of how closely those three are linked. I can't hold a negative thought, while I am celebrating a victory with a co-worker.

My Story:

I learned the value of rewarding myself, while I was a student being taught how to fly helicopters in Fort Rucker, Alabama. I will freely admit that this was a time where I was doing an incredible thing and getting paid for it. The schooling there is intense. We had military based classes, about flights, tactics, aerodynamics, weather, airspace, Federal Aviation Administration rules and even classes on basic leadership and conduct. The term they loved to use at Fort Rucker is that it is like trying to drink from a firehose. It is an excellent description. Student pilots are so overwhelmed, that if they are picking up 50% of the material presented they are doing incredibly well.

Everyone had to study to keep up, even the smartest among us. It equaled out to us working 5-6 days, with each day working 10-12 hours with study time on top of that. Although it was very exciting and a great career opportunity, it started to wear me down. Like many of the others, I was working that kind of grueling schedule and then coming home to a wife and children. While at home, I mostly ignored them and studied. It was the start of a downward spiral for me. I felt guilty about having to study and not spending time with my kids. When I diverted my attention to them, it felt great but my schooling suffered. As a result, the Army took more time from me for "study guidance." I started to only see the bad in everything or felt that any event was going to have a negative impact on me.

Fortunately, I have always had a solid mentor in my life. My dad told me that I was going to have to let some things slide in favor of others. Whichever I chose, school was only going to last another eight months. His suggestion was: "You're studying to be a pilot aren't you? Then "Winging" the test tomorrow should be simple. Take the kids out for pizza and ice cream and forget about it for a while. You've done great so far, it's now time to reward yourself."

It was a bizarre bit of advice from the endless energy supply, who is my father. I almost didn't take it. I'm so glad that I did. I played with my kids at a pizza and play house and didn't worry about the test. The next morning, I had accepted that I was going to receive a poor grade on the exam and was OK with it. I thought to myself that extra training be damned. As I rolled into the classroom, more relaxed and happier than I had been in a while, one of my classmates asked. "What the hell are you so happy about? This test is going to be brutal." I just shrugged and told him that I bailed on studying to take my kids out for pizza. He looked at me like I had lost my mind. Then he said, "We'll all be in retraining together I guess," and walked off. I laughed. It was so ridiculously out of character for me to not study, study, study, that everything seemed bizarre.

As I walked into the classroom, I noticed it was a beautiful day and that the room smelled like gummy bears! I could sense that this fine day was also going to include a hell of a thunderstorm. You could see the distant clouds and smell the rain miles away. I thought for a few seconds that I might have suffered a mental breakdown of some kind. I wasn't dreading the future or worried about the lack of study. I accepted it all calmly and the day just kept getting better and better. I wanted to do the test immediately, so that it could be over with and I could get back to enjoying the day. I was relaxed when they passed out the test papers and I started right away. I knew every answer but one. It all came easily to me. I was the first in the class to finish by a large margin. I couldn't believe it. Something had happened. I called my dad. He just laughed and said: "Everyone needs a break to reset their brains and to have some fun in their lives." That is when I started looking at how I had fared during the course of my schooling. I realized that stress and fatigue aren't the road to success and I need to take the time to find the good stuff in my life.

I also realized that those in study groups were doing better overall. I had been invited to join one like everyone, but only a few people ever spent much time in the groups. I started joining them. They set limits on the time they studied. They broke down the assignments. Everyone worked on a piece and then spent a few minutes explaining the answer and where they found it. We took breaks and celebrated when someone solved a complicated problem correctly. The student running it would throw out jolly ranchers or other small candies to everyone as rewards.

If someone from the study groups answer ended up being wrong, that person would correct the group the next day. The team excelled, and we were routinely at the top of the class. It freed up what felt like massive amounts of my time, since the study sessions had previously established stop times that were strictly enforced by the group.

After going it solo for the first part of flight training, I saw the enormous benefits of a group effort. I saw how using my extra time to keep my home support network happy and to keep my network of friends in contact, improved my life. I also learned a valuable lesson about taking breaks to "recharge" your mind and the value of a small reward for a solid effort. As addicted to self-improvement as I am, I spent some time after the kids went to bed studying why we need breaks, and what sleep does for learning and better study habits. Through that experience, I have learned that the value of the reward and celebration exercise is more about training yourself to look for the positives, than they are about the reward or celebration. If we keep looking for a reason to reward, we will find it and deserve it. It will change your outlook on life in general. There are too many good things happening, for it not to be a happy life.

CHAPTER FIVE

Giving and Self Improvement

The Concept:

LONG-LASTING HAPPINESS REQUIRES more than facing your daily life head-on with a smile. You can go for extended periods of time being perfectly happy without a purpose and without improving yourself or giving back to others. Eventually you are going to feel that something is missing. You need to find something which provides you with that missing sense of fulfillment. Giving back to others through charity or aid are remarkably fulfilling and isn't at all time-consuming. Self-improvement, whether it is seeking enlightenment or higher education, can also be a rewarding choice. The best and most lasting option is to find your purpose. It is the desire that lights you on fire with motivation to change things or even the world. Giving to others, self-improvement and finding purpose are as enhancing to happiness as frosting is to a cake.

What do you have to do?

Giving back is, by far, the easiest option to take. You probably have time left today to do something. Giving back can be done quickly.

You can donate time, money, ideas, or any of your talents or skills. The idea is simple. It is to help someone or something outside of your close-knit group, and to expect nothing in return.

Self-improvement is self-defined and is a broad subject. The main areas that people tend to improve themselves on are fitness, health, knowledge, state of mind, or skill sets. The desire to improve oneself is something that many of us seem to feel deeply. It can sometimes be all-consuming. You may feel unsettled if you're not learning or making aspects of your life better. The desire to improve yourself can be a driving force behind our actions in all aspects of our lives. One of the things I love about self-improvement is that it makes me focus my mind on the now and the present moment, almost as well as meditation. You can improve anything about yourself or your life. It can range from low-self-esteem to finding out how your brain works. Find something that you would like to make better in your life and dive in. The work is its own reward.

Finding purpose isn't as easily done as the other two. However, it does provide the longest and most rewarding life benefits. One of the hardest parts of finding your "purpose" is the preconceived ideas people have when you talk about purpose. It can include the images of

Mother Teresa, Gandhi or even people smashing tiny motorboats into huge whaling vessels. What we need to do is define what purpose is and then get you on a path toward it.

The general definition of purpose is an idea that you are passionate about that contributes or improves something outside of self. Saving Whales, Feeding the Hungry, Reaching Enlightenment, Congo Cat Cuddles or teaching people to dance are all examples of what your purpose could be. Finding that one thing that will drive you forward in your everyday life, is a task that can take some time. It will pay you back with an incredible sense of fulfillment. Once found and linked to your goals, your purpose will supercharge your life like never before.

How do I do it?

Giving back is definitely the simplest and quickest of these options. We can give back in so many small ways, that it can be hard to know where to start. It also varies greatly on what you currently do.

- A mother might volunteer at her children's school.

- A plumber might volunteer to repair elderly or low-income housing.

- A banker might do free financial counseling.

Most of us start with a more general giving back. We donate. Donating is giving back, many charities rely on this form of giving to impact our world. Just make sure that you do some research to ensure that your dollars are helping the cause, not the cause's staff.

There are some amazing charities out there. The Combined Federal Campaign is one resource that can help you find the charity close to your heart. The charities listed on the site are audited and have to report their operating costs vs actual aid given percentage to the list.

https://cfctoday.org/who-is-in-the-campaign   is where the annual list usually can be found. My favorite part is that they are color coded for ease. It allows me to see which charities have the highest staffing costs. The CFC requires them to disclose that number. It is listed for every charity in the corner as an AFR. AFR stands for Administrative and Fundraising Rate, which is listed with an organization's other information. The AFR is the percentage of donation dollars that are spent on administration costs. This represents the overhead costs of an organization.

For example, if a charity has an AFR of 8%, 8 cents of every received dollar covers the administrative overhead costs while 92 cents goes to services provided by the organization. In this case, 92% of your dollars go to the actual 'helping'. Some of the listed and popular charities have appalling numbers. If it is 8% or less, then they are doing great. If it was 12% for a charity I supported, it wouldn't phase me. If it was much higher than that, I would have to put some serious thought into it.

Donating food or other articles is another way to provide help. I recommend church and school drives for this, whenever possible. Nearly all of what you donate will go to those in need. Most of the time your aid stays local so it's a favorite way to give. There are other options as well. The little old lady down the street might like to have her yard mowed. The park might need a little extra litter control. A friend might need a meal cooked for them, while they are ill. I also love the random acts of kindness that can be done almost everywhere. Pay the toll for the guy behind you or buy coffee for a stranger. Giving back is never out of place, so get creative.

I love to read stories about people doing things for others. Tell it on the social media of your choice. Getting the word out on giving gives us all a boost.

Self-improvement

We are so lucky to be living in these exciting times. We literally have the resources at our fingertips to learn and develop in just about anything we can think of. The internet has revolutionized our lives and gives everyone the opportunity to learn. It is an incredible time to be a human being who is seeking to better yourself. There are so many ways that you can immediately improve your life.

How would you like to start an exercise regimen? There are 31,500,000 web returns on "how to build a workout plan." The biggest problem with exercising, isn't the plan or knowledge or even the doing. It is choosing which expert advice to follow. There are even exercise fanatics with their own clubs and near cult like followings now. Join and become one of the incredibly in shape diehards, like a P90X'er or the current king of workout cults, the Crossfitter.   Both of those close-knit groups have a lot going for them and have large followings and support systems.   Some of them include fantastic and thorough exercise guides, inexpensive training facilities and the support of the team.

Although I am not a member, I know many who are. They continually talk about the community of fellow exercisers rooting for them and pushing them toward the next goal. That can be a great experience, and for those of us without a lot of motivation, it can be vital.

If that level of intensity doesn't appeal to you, there are millions of other exercise options. The most important part is to be real with yourself and to set workout goals by writing them down for you and/or others to see. As with all goal setting it is important to be realistic with your goals.   Going from lifting 60 kg (132lbs) to 160 kg (352lbs) doesn't happen in a month.   Neither does running 2k (1.25miles) to running 12k (7.5miles). Figure out exactly what you want to achieve. Do you want to be fit at 50? Do you want to lose some of those extra pounds? Whatever it is, write it down and then select the right workout plan, diet and schedule. Don't get too caught up in the 31 million options, pick something reputable and stick to it. When setting workout goals use the SMART goal building system, it's a proven goal setting aid that works no matter what you goal is. The SMART acronym for goal setting consists of:

Specific- The goal must be as specific as possible. Write down - I want to run 8 km in 45 minutes NOT I want to run faster and in a quicker time.

Measurable-Or even quantifiable, you can measure 8 km but faster than what? More than who?

Attainable-Are you in a situation where it is possible to run 8 km? Are your legs and knees in working order? Is 8 km in 45 minutes a reasonable time for a human? Look it up on the internet. Research your goal.

Realistic-Can you make the time, produce the effort and commit enough to make it happen?

Timeframe-How much time are you giving yourself? You should be realistic and specific.

If your goal passes the smart test, we end with a written goal like this:

'I want to run 8 km in 45 minutes by the August 23rd this year.'

This is a workable goal. However, if you stop there you will most likely not reach it. You need to dive deeper to make each step actionable. Some people like goals inside of goals. I prefer calling them actionable steps. There are many great ways to do this. I will share with you the U.S. Army thoughts on goal setting that have served me well for many years.

Goal: Run 8 k in 45 Minutes by August 23rd

Step 1. Time an 8 k run/walk

Result: 58 minutes

(Then you implement your plan, whatever the web or a smart trainer has for you.)

Week 1 Run 3 times 4 k fast, 8 k jog, 10 k slow
Week 2 Run 3 times 4 k fast, 8 k jog, 10 k slow
Week 3 Run 2 times 4 k fast, 8 k for time goal 50 minutes
Week 4 Run 3 times 4 k fast, 6 k jog, 8 k for time
Week 5 Run 3 times 4 k fast, 6 k jog, 8 k for time
Week 6 Run 2 times 4 k fast, 6 k jog, 8 K in 45 minutes

Goal achieved! Reward yourself!!

This is not the workout plan I am suggesting to anyone. It is just a way to demonstrate breaking down a larger goal into actionable steps. These actionable steps remove the intimidation factor of larger goals. Smaller steps towards your goals seem easier to accomplish. Therefore, they require less of your precious willpower to achieve. Don't let Quitter's dip knock you off your goals! Here is what quitters dip looks like:

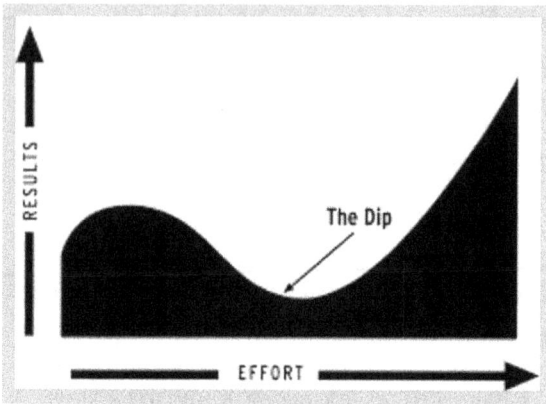

Quitter's dip is a term used to describe the trends when people quit. At first, we are highly motivated and are being spurred on by the newness of what we have undertaken. As the newness wears off, the motivation drops sharply. We end up in the dip, before we ever start seeing decent results. This is the time when 80% of people quit on a project or self-improvement routine. If they could have just managed their willpower a little more, it would have kept them from being affected by the dip. The results would have started to come, which would have provided additional motivation to continue. I've also heard it called the hump or the wall. If you stick with it, you will start seeing greater benefits from your efforts.

Identifying where you are in the dip, can be a huge help in getting through it. Once you know where you are, if you stick it out a bit longer the dip seems easier to get through. Another way to help you get through the dip, is to add a new element to the program or routine. Add a new reward to the middle of a new run route or a new anything and get the will to keep going from the excitement of doing a new thing.

Self-improvement isn't just limited to exercise. It can include many different things. I routinely work on Mindsets, traditional education style topics (math, language and writing), broadening horizons, enlightenment and hands-on skills. Like my apocalypse loving friend says.

"He who can make booze and bacon will rule the world!"

I now know how to do both, because I love learning new things. It has nothing to do with fearing zombies (hence the stock pile of bacon!) or any love for alcohol, it's just fun to learn. As I so excitedly proclaimed earlier, there has never been a better time to learn anything. There are more options than are possible to list. Therefore, I will just include the ones that I personally have used with fantastic results.

My number one place to learn how to do anything is youtube.com. If there isn't a video about it already on youtube, reconsider what you are trying to do. It might be illegal! The hardest part is sorting through the garbage to get to the gold, but it is in there.

Websites such as Instructables and Wikihow are specifically there to show you how to do just about anything. If you want to improve your kid's costume, make a backyard grill, run a Christmas light extravaganza, or even program, then these websites have you covered.

What if you want to open your mind to science and

the larger world? TedTalks, BBC Learning, and BigTh-ink can give it to you in short bursts to truly amaze and enlighten you. How about absolutely top tier classes? Have you tried Yale's Open Courses yet? How about Open University in the UK? If not, head over to take a look at what they are offering free of charge. There is a surprisingly long list of some of the best education programs in the world.

More of a Harvard or MIT type? They also offer free courses through Harvard's Open Learning and MIT's Open Courseware or even Stanford Online. I couldn't be more in love with Harvard's set, but all of these institutions' classes are of the superb caliber that you would expect from such prestigious schools.

If you are looking for a broader range of topics, you can go to Coursera. Lectures from dozens of schools are free, or you can even sign up for a fee and get a certificate for completing a course.

Switching gears again, are you searching for enlightenment? In addition to the stacks of videos and guides on several of the websites listed above, there are free ebooks to download to the Kindle app which you can get for your desktops, laptops, smartphones, tablets and kindle readers. For a few bucks, you can buy a self-help book on just about any topic. If you prefer to listen to material rather than read, you can get an audiobook and squeeze some reading in on the drive to work.

Do foreign Languages tickle your fancy? There are many apps out there for learning a language. You will have difficulty choosing which one to download. I like Duolingo, Learn (fill in language), Memrise and Chineseskill. Although this isn't a list book, I wanted to impress upon you, how many excellent options are available to you. If you want to be better, then the resources are available. Avoid "quitters dip" and there is nothing you can't achieve.

How to determine and define purpose.

"Your purpose in life is to find your purpose and give your whole heart and soul to it."
— **Gautama Buddha**
"If you want to live a happy life, tie it to a goal, not to people or things."
— **Albert Einstein**
"There is no greater gift you can give or receive than to honor your calling. It's why you were born. And how you become most truly alive."
— **Oprah Winfrey**
"The two most important days in your life are the day you are born and the day you find out why."
— **Mark Twain**

I could fill this book just with quotes of the greatest minds and thinkers about their opinions on purpose. It is that important. Purpose is probably already driving your life in one way or another. It is there, you just need to define it to start reaping the huge benefits you get from having a purpose.

The importance of having purpose obviously isn't a new concept. Why then is purpose not a straightforward thing to teach someone how to find in their life? If everyone had the same values experiences, interests and background, it would still be hard to formulate a step by step guide on how to define their purpose. I am going to present basic steps to help you. I do understand that my process may not work for everyone. In the end, I will give you some other options that I have found interesting to help you on your path. **It is that important.** It should be a priority on your list of things to do. Once you find your purpose, it will quickly change your life for the better. It will transform how you feel and how you live.

What a PURPOSE should be.

1. I like Patrick McKnight and Todd Kashdan's definition of 'purpose' the best. They define it this way-

   "Purpose is defined as a central, self-organizing life aim. Central in that if present, purpose is a predominant theme of a person's identity. If we envision a person positioning descriptor of their personality on a dartboard, purpose would be near the innermost, concentric circle."

   Using this definition, we learn that purpose should be an idea, concept or have a broad scope to it. There should be no reasonable way that you can fail at your purpose, because it is a part of your identity. If it is a powerful enough reason to call you to action, it should propel you to put maximum effort into it. It will help to determine your goals and drive your decisions toward achieving them. "Getting an A on my final" or "Cleaning up my neighborhood park" are not purposes, they are goals. This doesn't mean that your purpose can't have an end state. Just that it isn't like to have one you can achieve in the near future, and even then may just be a refocusing point instead of a real end. As an example "Save the Whales," one of the more publicized goals of whale enthusiasts is the interception of whaling vessels. It is possible that someday whaling will be illegal. This would be a huge victory, but it would not be the end of the purpose for those who tirelessly fight for the whales. There would still be garbage in the Pacific that could affect the health of whales. There could also be the illegal whaling that would occur. A worldwide whaling ban would just shift the focus from people on boats charging at the harpoons to people standing on the Pacific Garbage Island. It is still worthy, still necessary and still striving to save the whales.

2. Your Purpose can be shared with others. However, it must be YOURs to own. It is also something you have to come up with yourself. It should affect you emotionally when you work on it. It doesn't need to be unique. Feeding hungry children is a purpose that many people feel a need to do. There are many who are actively involved in achieving this purpose. It is

a grand and noble purpose. It benefits from having facilities that are already in place for you to start supporting with time and effort. This allows you to get out into the community to help without the hassle of starting with no direction.

3. A Purpose should add value to a group, community or the world. Your purpose is like art and religion. It must support your beliefs and be amazing to you. You may only affect a few but that will be enough to change lives and to motivate others to follow their own paths. It will allow you to be the person that everyone wants to be like. In this manner, you also teach others as you learn your own way through your life purpose.

What a Purpose should not be:

1. You are not the purpose. It cannot be anything that only results in personal benefit. Gaining from your purpose is fantastic, but personal gain cannot be your purpose. If you can make a living striving toward your purpose, I recommend that you do it immediately! Artists make money from the paintings that they sell, while the buyer receives a piece of beauty they can look at forever. A life coach receives money for teaching people better strategies to move forward. The person being coached may achieve their own purpose through the help of their coach. Those are just a couple examples of people fulfilling their purpose and making money while they do.

2. It should not have a finish line, or one that can be easily reached. It should also not be quick. Those are called goals. I love them, but they are different from your purpose. It can be subtle as the difference between cleaning your neighborhood park and improving neighborhood parks. One can be done in a weekend or two and is definitely worth doing. The other is a process that requires thought, time and effort to make the most substantial improvements possible. Life purpose is just that – for life. It should be something that doesn't feel like work or a chore. It should come naturally to you and be something that you could never think of giving up. This means that there is no retirement date.

3. A purpose is not about devoting your life to a person. We all have those who we love, but they are not a purpose. Even raising children as a purpose should be approached with caution. It's hard to set an example of living a life with purpose to your kids, when you are defining them as your purpose. They are much less likely to view themselves as a purpose than you are. It is possible, but you should be careful.

How to find and then define your Purpose.

I am going to give you a few options. These are things that I believe will at least help start you on the right path.

Option #1

What are you very good at? What are you passionate about? What makes your blood boil, or your tears fall? What makes you focus so intently, that the rest of the world disappears? When was the last time you hopped out of bed because you were happy to do something important?

These are great first questions to ask yourself while trying to figure out your purpose. Examine your answers and compare them to the lists of what may and may not be a Purpose.

My answers to the above questions:

I am an experienced and competent instructor. I love to write. It upsets me to see so many people who do not feel happiness in their lives. The world disappears when I play Pacman! I pop out of bed nearly every day because I love greeting my days with enthusiasm.

You can see my purpose in the answers to those questions. My actual answers are quite a bit longer. I am sure that yours will be too. If you answer honestly, your purpose is likely to be on that list. Think about what it is you could do with each of those points listed to make the difference you want to make. After you think about them, try to find the one that stirs your emotions the most. It will be the one that you can see yourself actively pursuing. Look at what is in the scope of your current ability. If you are certain that you have found the right

Purpose and feel it is outside of your current ability to achieve, consider promoting awareness, while building the skills you need. This can be done on all the social media and in most schools and communities. You might be surprised at the level of support you get once you start. I certainly was.

Other questions that might help:

What service can I give to help others?

When was the last time I felt empowered by something I did?

Who do I feel inspired by?

Why are they inspiring?

What is it I love to do? (listen carefully to the first answer your mind gives you)

What could I do for the rest of my life that would never feel like work and I would want to do every day of my life?

Option #2

Research! There are many fantastic causes in the world. They include: the eradication of diseases, helping children in every way imaginable, helping people, animal causes, saving trees, saving oceans, preserving history, preserving knowledge, religious causes, etc... It can seem overwhelming but just takes a little time to get through.

If one of these captured your interest, then you have a starting point. Research it! The great part of finding purpose this way is that you could find an organization to help start you on the path. They can educate you and often have ways on their websites, where you can start helping right away. Beware of those that only have the "Donate" feature on the web. Most of the organizations that are making real change have more to them than a donation site.

Start getting involved in whatever you can right away. If the cause stirs you enough but the organization doesn't, find your own path or a new group. Better yet, start a new group.

Remember, we all have strengths so use yours today.

What if nothing is standing out yet? You should consider joining something that appeals to you, even if it isn't striking you as the right "one." It could lead to something else that does stir you. Sometimes the first thing you think is your purpose may not be the one you stick with. It can sometimes be a journey and different paths open up to you just by trying. Don't grow despondent. You might have to try out a few things before you find your true purpose. Don't let people judge you for trying out new things. If people say you're being fickle and never stick with anything, tell them you are just not happy to settle until you find the right thing. It's a task worthy of the search.

Option #3

Ok! Take a deep breath. Here comes the standard 'Lee' answer to everything: Meditate on it. That is how I found my purpose. If that isn't up your alley, pray on it. It doesn't matter if you pray to the Angels, God, Ganesha, Buddha, The Universe, The Field of Potentiality, or the Cosmic Spaghetti Monster. - If you clear and open your mind to the answer, it will come.

It isn't an instant solution. It can take time. Once I identified that my life was missing something important, it hit me like a school bus. I asked and got ran over by the answer. It was like it was just waiting for me to open the door to the possibility. We have many distractions in our lives. They include schedules and deadlines, traffic and frustration, other people texting and talking and ads and worries. They all buzz inside your mind until they are deliberately silenced. Once it is quiet, it takes a few sessions just to relax and receive. There are many things you could do to add fulfillment to your life. All that you have to do is ask yourself and pick the best one.

Once you have figured out your Purpose, you should make it into a statement. Transforming that deep gut feeling of capital "P" Purpose into a statement will help you gain the most benefit and focus your efforts on achieving it. Imagine someone asking you what your purpose is. Write down the answer that will make you proud to say. You are also going to want to write it out as to help you goal build toward your purpose. The statement is for you, so it should speak to you in some way. Play with it a little, until it sounds right. Here is mine:

> I will make my world better. (How it impacts) I will teach people the knowledge and skills to lead a consistently happy life. (Statement of Purpose) I know them well, implement them daily and consider myself an expert on the topic. (Why this Purpose is mine)

When linked to the goals in your life, your Purpose will add new motivation to accomplish them. It suddenly becomes a pleasure to work towards your goals. It will also add fulfillment to your daily life, when you see that the work you do is linked to something greater. That is a huge step toward consistent happiness. This topic is so important, that if you did not find this section helpful, I have listed several other options below to help you on your path. I want you to feel fulfilled. I believe finding that important thing you do with your life is essential.

If the three options above don't appeal to you, try reading one of the articles below.

https://markmanson.net/life-purpose
Mark gives us an often crude but humorous look that sounds very anti-purpose but could be helpful anyway.

http://www.lifecoachspotter.com/what-is-your-purpose-in-life/
They are selling a product. This article is metaphor heavy!

It is well thought out and is a different approach that might work for you.

https://www.wakeupcloud.com/secret-to-finding-your-life-purpose/
Short with similar recommendations to option 3, so obviously I like it.

https://www.ted.com/playlists/313/talks_to_help_you_find_your_pu
TED Talks- I am a huge fan. I find these insightful and entertaining. It may help you to hear other people's stories, though it isn't necessarily a guide.

Why Should I Do It?

Why does giving unto others work? It is survival of the fittest, right? Despite hearing that phrase over and over again, it doesn't work that way in society. It doesn't even make sense to think that way. Thankfully we are and have always been social beings. We take care of our young, and babies aren't what I would call the fittest. Our communities have served us throughout human history, we are hardwired for them. For many the feeling of community is starting to fragment. How many people know and love their neighbor? When was the last time you gave your neighbor anything beyond a semi-friendly wave? Just because we no longer need the physical security and the shared food gathering of the group, it does NOT mean that we have lost our instinctual need for community. It has left many of us feeling the vacuum in our lives. It is the vacuum where we gave freely and received gratefully. Facebook's success alone is proof of the human drive toward the community.

In a Harvard University study focusing on children's performance in school, they found that children who were happy, scored far better. They also discovered was that happy children had several critical things in common. They had a strong connection to family AND a strong connection to a group of their peers. Those micro-communities, even in school, were helping us in a variety of ways. The shared interests tie us together, and the giving and receiving in the group enhances the children in it.

We thrived in communities. They provided us with ample opportunity to give and get a feeling of belonging in return. The community itself contributes new ideas, fresh laughter and much more.

Research has shown that giving makes us far happier than receiving. Numerous studies have shown that giving money to charities or to others in need, will make you happier than spending it on yourself. Professor Michael Norton of Harvard University questioned over 600 Americans about their income and what they spent their money on. He then asked them to rate how happy they felt on a daily basis. He found that, regardless of income, those who spent more money on others than themselves were decidedly happier. Real wealth has nothing to do with what you own. It is about the feeling of fulfillment that you have in your life. There are not many things in this life that will lead you to that feeling, more than making a noticeable difference in someone else's life.

What does happiness have to do with self-improvement? We first need a foundation. A key ingredient to that foundation is healthy self-esteem. Once we increase our self-esteem and learn to value ourselves, it becomes easier to have increased happiness throughout the day. Creating a healthy sense of self-esteem can be a lot of work for many of us. Part of it is the acceptance we discussed earlier. From that acceptance, we often get a good look at the things in our life that we need to improve. Self-improvement and healthier self-esteem are partners that help each other to advance. On the other hand, unchecked low self-esteem leads to mental health issues, such as anxiety and depression. It sometimes has tragic results and perpetuates a life of misery. A UC Davis Medical Center paper on self-esteem found: "A person with low self-esteem feels unworthy, incapable, and incompetent." One of their recommendations for improving low self-esteem is to do affirmations and I am a huge fan of this advice. We will discuss affirmations in the next chapter. They also recommended seeking self-improvement in any aspect of your life. Once you start a journey of self-improvement, it is easy to see the value that you have. It shows that you are smart enough and good enough to make a difference. It can improve how you look at yourself. It can also create a strong foundation of happiness in your life and help you find greater purpose.

The science of purpose is still relatively new. Having a purpose is linked to having a longer life, according to a large study in *The Lancet*. They studied people claiming to have a life purpose and an increased sense of well-being that was linked to it. They then compared them with a group that had no life purpose and observed them over the next eight years. They found that the people with purpose had a 30% lower chance of dying over the eight years, even after eliminating many exogenous factors such as smoking, wealth or physical activity. If you don't eliminate those factors it reported a staggering 58% lower mortality rate than the non-purpose group. Purpose improves the lives of those that have a defined one. It provides a sense of well- being and a healthier self-esteem. It also solidifies peoples' concept of who they are. It drives you toward goals that result in giving and improving yourself. Purpose helps you make sound decisions about your health, since being unhealthy inhibits your ability to serve your purpose. Though the science is still unsure on the why, the observed results are not in question. People with purpose live longer, healthier and happier lives.

My Story:

I do all of these things. I am a self-proclaimed self-improvement junkie! I consume self-help books like the pages are made of cake. Audible is currently my primary means or reading self-help, since I do so much traveling. There is nothing like listening to lectures about the frontal cortex changing internal structures, while I speed down the freeway.

I also read studies on happiness, learning, psychology and spirituality. I can't get enough of them fit into my day! My father once gave me a book to read It was called *Rhinoceros Success* by Scott Alexander. It is a short book, which I thought was a bit silly. However, my father got great delight out of it and often told me so. I didn't care for it much, because at the time I was a junior non-commissioned officer and was feeling entirely powerless in my job. I had told my father how I felt. According to the book, I was a cow, who was happily grazing away, making no waves and enjoying few successes. It took me longer than I care to admit to see what my father had been up to. I can still remember him yelling CHARGE like a rhino and laughing! It was the perfect advice for me at the time, wrapped in a book and given to me by my greatest advisor.

Taking action, making decisions and going for it was the advice that saved my Army career. Only a year later, I was selected to join the best 1% of the army, the ever humble, always correct, beloved Warrant Officer Corps. Just before that hectic adventure started, I got another book from dad, 'Who Moved My Cheese' by Dr. Spencer Johnson. Just like that, I was hooked. 'Rhinoceros Success' reappeared in my life recently as a prerequisite to my current job. I can't believe I ever thought it was a silly book.

The love of learning runs deep in all of us. There is a jolt of joy after discovery and a buzz in implementing new ideas into our lives. I love it not because of a feeling that I desperately need to be better, but because each step of learning anything feels fulfilling.

The self-help books soon led me into many other training events. It was primarily military professional training. There were also classes from a variety of colleges and universities on whatever topic seemed interesting. Once the internet became widespread, it served as a teacher and introduced me to a wide range of courses. I can't think of a time when I wasn't actively in the process of learning something new. The online courses have made such enormous improvements recently. I expect that there will be a Universal University with full interactive classroom environments and the best professors and instructors in the world available with just a few clicks within the next few years. I'm very excited about it. There are nearly limitless opportunities to improve our society.

Along my path, I found the only thing more satisfying than learning was instructing. Something that I had loved doing as a Sergeant in the Army, was teaching Officer Candidate School classes or teaching my own soldiers in Air Traffic Control or other common soldiering skills. My love of learning and teaching eventually led me to the Instructor Pilot Course and the Instrument Evaluator's Course. With this remarkable training under my belt, I shifted my study to concentrate on teaching and instruction. The classes became even more rewarding, since I could put new techniques and discoveries into action almost immediately.

A couple of years into that cycle, I started taking classes and reading more on psychology in order to make me a better instructor. During my courses in that particular field, I stumbled on a study by HGSE lecturer Christina Hinton about student happiness and how it affected their learning. The article spoke to me and the study findings were surprising. It turns out that happiness improves study and performance more than I had ever imagined. I was intrigued. I dove into everything I could study, read or watch on the topic of happiness and performance. I had always been told by people that I was the happiest person they knew. The happiness theme resonated with me, I had found my purpose.

I continue to read and devour, anything that I can find on happiness. After I transitioned out of the military, I was looking for my next step, when the happiness bug caught me again during meditation. I had a strong sense that I should share what I had learned with others and encourage them to share it with even more people. The book is just a part of my effort to spread the word and get you and those like you, to help each other on your unique path to happiness. There will be times when something makes you sad or mad, but you won't linger there long before returning to being happy. That is what it means to have happiness as your baseline, join me there and bring everyone with you. It's a super great way to live.

CHAPTER SIX

Staking Your Claim

PRO-CLAIM, LAY CLAIM, and ex-claim

The Concept:

You must choose or claim happiness in your life in order to make it your baseline, your default setting.

What do you have to do?

You must start spending time living in the Now. Most of us spend more time thinking about the future or reliving and regretting the past, than we do living in the present moment.

Understand that you have choices. They are yours to make. To make it easier to choose, we need to affirm our worth and goals.

Wake up and claim your happy and seize this day!

How do I do it?

How in the heck do I NOT live in the present is the first thing most people ask when I talk about living in the now. For starters, this is not a requirement to achieve lasting happiness. It is more like the key to unshakable happiness and a sense of well-being. Living in the present is the thing that brings me the most consistent stream of happy thoughts and pleasures in my life.

To take this path, you must first accept that you are more than just your thoughts. That is a concept that threw me off at first. If you were your thoughts, then every time you regretted something you'd done in the past you would be magically teleported back to the past to "Do it right." Then you would teleport straight into the future, like some terrible but very addictive sci-fi novel, to handle all those things that you are worrying about in the future. When we allow ourselves to only occupy those two states we become unproductive and unhappy. Likewise, if fear of the future and regret over the past is all that motivates you to act in the present then happiness will continue to elude you.

Letting your thoughts inhabit the future through worry, frets, or anticipation causes constant anxiety. When you combine the time we spend dwelling in the past and fantasizing about the future, how much time is left? For most of us, the answer is not much. The times we do spend in the present moment are fleeting. It amounts to a few instances at a time when savoring something we enjoy or where tragedy strikes. It's like when you nearly have an accident in a car and time apparently slows down, allowing you to make the necessary corrections instinctively. In moments like this the brain shuts down those worries and upsets leaving the full capacity of your mind to work the problem. Living in the moment can also be when you focus fully on every aspect of a fabulous meal. It's where your senses are all reporting in, and you are taking notice of it. It is very exhilarating and calming. It is also very hard to imagine, until you've been there a few times yourself. It is why so many of us get addicted to thrill-seeking and intense exercise routines.

It is our natural instinct to shut those outside thoughts down while we do those things. We only take notice of the present moment. The actor, Will Smith, was speaking of his skydiving adventure, when he nailed it with this quote:

> *"You realize that the point of maximum danger*
> *is the point of minimum fear."*

That is a perfect description of living the moment. There is no fear, no worry, no sadness and no upsets at all. There is just acceptance of the moment and wonder at how great everything is.

There are some spectacular additional reads out there on living in the present moment. I will list several at the end of this section if you would like some additional information. We are going to look at some ways to live in the moment which we can implement and which will allow us to see results relatively quickly. The first step is to define what is meant by presence. Presence is total body awareness. All of the senses acknowledged and alive. Smell, taste, feeling, sight and sounds are all registered. Your thoughts are not in the future or the past, because neither of them exists in the moment.

I initially found it very difficult to find presence for any length of time. I could only find it during meditation. However, that isn't exactly what we are talking about. Presence is more like that feeling of being still and quiet, even though you are interacting with the world. By contrast, during meditation you are just still and quiet. Living in the now is one of those simple things that has become hard for us, after years of building bad habits.

It's easy to focus on what is happening right now, but it is very hard to stay that way for long. Our minds continuously throw new thoughts at us. It creates tangent tales about what is happening in our lives and tries to play them to us and wash away the focus that we are trying to attain. We have to accept and acknowledge the thoughts or label them and push them aside. The more we do it, the easier it becomes. The change from hard to easy comes quickly within a week of practice. It sounds counter-intuitive, but when we possess the moment, the answers to our hardest questions will emerge.

Once we've weeded out our unnecessary and distracting thoughts, we give that mental processing power over to the now. Whether you believe the answer comes to you because you are quiet enough to hear it from an outside source or that you have given your mind the space it needs to resolve the issue doesn't matter. The problems ARE easier to solve, the feelings ARE happier and the world IS more vibrant. Who doesn't want that in their life? It's a fantastic experience available to anyone in the world. Try it out!

> *"The secret of health for both mind and body is not to mourn for the past, worry about the future, or anticipate troubles, but to live in the **present moment** wisely and earnestly."*
> *~ Buddha.*

Here are a few steps to help you on the path.

1. **ACCEPTANCE** -You know those feelings of anger, regret, shame, and disappointment? We've all suffered from one upset or another. When someone chastises you for something you didn't feel was wrong, you might feel anger towards the other person and then at yourself for letting that person make you angry. These double whammies linger far longer than accepting the fact that you are angry. If you let yourself experience the emotion, moving on becomes easier when you are ready.

   You must also realize that regardless of the nature of the upset (such as fear, worry, anger, etc.) they have an important thing in common. The events causing them are in the past or in the future. They are rather over and can't be changed or have yet to happen. To dwell on things by rehashing, reviewing, and spending hours contemplating about them, is doing you harm. It can sometimes be a considerable harm. If you made an error, accept that you made it and then forgive yourself. Let the emotion run its course. You shouldn't judge it, hold onto it or push it away. Acceptance goes beyond the forgiveness we worked on in an earlier chapter. It is also seeing the present moment and acknowledging it as the truth. Accept your circumstance as this moment's truth and move on. As the thoughts of past and future happen, remember they are only thoughts. Let them happen and end. I find it helpful to give them no more attention than a quick labeling. Usually I label them as past, future, anger and absurdity. A quick "that already happened, it's the past," then moving on. Once the thoughts have been identified like that they are easier to put aside, and quickly retreat from your mind.

2. **SAVOR**- Practice living in the present by finding something to savor. Foodies and wine devotees rejoice, many of you have already trained yourself to take in every aspect of the experience. When I go to the beach, I let the whole scene sink in. I smell the salty water, I feel the sand between my toes and fingers, I taste my beverage of choice and I listen to the sounds of the gulls and the waves crashing. I don't think about my work tomorrow or my fender bender that happened yesterday. I also don't worry about getting the best spot or being too close or too far from anyone. I accept the circumstances and my

enjoyment skyrockets. My happiness bursts forth in smiles, and I feel more alive than I ever could outside the moment. The out of their time thoughts still try to invade. If it is not their moment or they don't belong, I label them, and they fade away.

3. **OBSERVE**- Stop what you are doing right now and look around you. Just take a minute to look at that incredible tree outside your window or that interesting building across the road. Observe your surrounding and allow all your senses to be exposed to the moment. Notice the smells, sounds, temperature and everything else! Let the moment wrap you up and take you with it. Let the flow around you guide your pace, whether in traffic, on the sidewalk or at work. Go in a different direction to work and look at the new sights, listen to some music and move with it. I love my drive to work more these days. Traffic backed up and running late is even better. I look at the other people in their cars frowning and upset. Do you think that upset is getting them to work any faster? That acidic attitude is going to eat through them all day. They are going to spread their negative funk to everyone they come into contact with. But not me. I hear the music and the beeps, smiling and waving at passers-by and thoroughly enjoying the moment. I go with the flow of traffic or lack of flow and it doesn't matter, you are going to be late or early regardless of the emotions you attach here so

choose to be happy. I am not telling you they are the best moments in my life, but they are good and I get enjoyment from them.

4. **JOURNALING**- I picked journaling up again after reading the fantastic "The Miracle Morning" by Hal Elrod. I had journaled a couple of times while deployed, but lost the habit when I returned to the U.S. Those of you who are familiar with Elrod's book, will see his influence in my journaling technique. What follows is the way I use my journal. What works for you may be something entirely different. In Jennie Moraitis's "Happy Journal Happy Life" she teaches you to draw and sketch your journal entries. It's a technique that can be quite addictive and I've even started including the occasional sketch in my own entries.

Journaling is a helpful review of yesterday's accomplishments and near-misses. I do not have to waste brainpower concerned about the previous day's follies, because I have addressed them in the morning in my journal. I also don't have to worry about today's actions, because I have also already laid those out in my journal. That is a present/mindfulness enabler for the rest of my day. There is no wondering or worrying about what I need to accomplish.

Journaling also opens up your thoughts and emotions in the moment. If right now I feel angry or sad or afraid or any other variety of upset, it gives me the quiet moments to feel that upset, identify the cause and accept it. Besides that journals are excellent ways to do the following:

1. Journaling is a way to write our goals and the review the progress we make toward achieving them. We can highlight the step by step of our pitfalls and successes. It becomes our way of refocusing effort and patting ourselves on the back for work well done.

2. Journals are a way to express feelings that you feel you can't share with others. Getting them down on paper (digital or otherwise) is a way to look at the problem in black and white. I find it much easier to problem solve when I have taken the step of clearly writing down the problem. The solutions seem to jump out at you after that.

3. It is an easy way to track your patterns of behavior. Have you been arguing a lot or having great days? Figuring out why either of these are occurring, can be truly enlightening.

4. My private journal provides me with accountability for my own actions and inactions. This is why I have become such a fan of journaling. I write down what I did yesterday and what I need to do today. It tracks my progress and has shown me what I can and can't accomplish. This assists me to set realistic goals.

5. The mental high fives for accomplishments and the expressions of gratitude are a reward for myself. It

reminds me that I am making progress and becoming better.

6. It becomes a sounding board for some of my most creative work. I jot, describe or detail what I have in mind and can then go back the next day, check if it still sounds valid, and then make adjustments or add-ons, when needed.

7. It is a storehouse for my most positive thoughts. I try and write one aphorism a day in it. There are some that I love and others I think are so-so. However, they are all positive thoughts. I go back and read them when I need a boost.

How to journal:

Do this in any manner that feels right to you and you can accomplish every day. The right answer is the one that works for you. I give myself ten minutes to do it each day. On non-work days I may write longer, but after ten minutes I am done most days. The entries aren't long. However, they are very helpful. It is a great start to a mindful day.

1. I picked a journal system/medium that works for me. I chose a standard cheap book with lines but no dates. I have also looked at some great online options or dated ones and passed. This is what fits my style. You can use apps or the note section on your smart phone or even Word on your computer.

There are many ways to record your thoughts.

2. I agreed to not care about sentence structure or spelling as long as the ideas were understandable. I also decided that there was no length limit on sentences, short or long.

3. I decided if I missed days I would leave pages blank as a reminder they happened and that I missed the everyday mark.

4. I structure all entries the same, although I am not a slave to it. The general format for me is:

How was yesterday? Why?
What am I grateful for?
What did I accomplish?
What did I mean to do but did not accomplish?
What ideas, comments, concerns or significant things
   do I feel I need to put down?
What do I need to get done today?
Positive statement about today.
Aphorism

5. The substance is more important than all of these ideas.

This is how I journal. It works really well for me and is worth the ten minutes I invest on most days. Some days, I only put down a brief statement. Other days, I go longer. I encourage you to play around with it until you find the sweet spot for you. I feel strongly about this outstanding tool for self-improvement. Journaling is the second most instantaneous help you can give yourself toward happiness after smiling. It takes just ten minutes and can improve your life and day. I've talked to people who think it is the most valuable part of their daily routine. Whether you buy a paper version, use an app start one today. Invest the few minutes and let me know how it is working for you. Claiming your happiness in written form is a great way to make it stick.

Waking up and claiming that you're happy is pretty easy. I wake up every day and start with my first affirmation, while still in bed. "Today is going to be a great day!" Or fantastic or amazing, you get what I mean. Claim it from the moment consciousness takes you! That way the universe, your partner, your children and most importantly YOU already know how this day is going to go down.

I love affirmations. This simple one is the most important for me. It has never failed me. Even when tragedy strikes, my affirmation that 'today is going to be great' shines through a winner. It helps keep my mind on the positive. The "We caught that before it could get much worse," attitude versus the "this is the worst thing ever to happen".

In addition to that first affirmation, I also have written affirmations that I read aloud each day. It has become an important part of my routine and sets the day up to be a positive all-round experience. Affirmations play a different role in your life than goals. Your goals are about where you want to be in two weeks, one month or five years in the future. Affirmations are about the present and my role in the present. Affirmations help prepare you for the day and remind you of your direction. They also pump daily vitality into your goals and help to keep you on track.

Affirmations are also a powerful tool to change your outlook, motivate you and alter emotions and thoughts. I consider them a powerhouse of personal transformation. The problem with finding a guide to affirmations is that they seem to be completely different in the description of use and the elements. All that data can get confusing. It doesn't matter too much because what works for you will be what you believe will work. Your belief is that powerful.

I am going to give you an example of two different and effective ways to write them. They can be as simple as one word if that works for you. The first one I consider is the "Napoleon Hill Method". This is an adaption from his original work - Think and Grow Rich. He was talking specifically about money, but I find that it also works for other things. Remember before starting, that ALL parts of affirmations should be positive statements about the now! "I am," not "I want to." "I am handsome!" not "I am going to stop being ugly!"

1. Fix in your mind exactly what you desire. It is not sufficient merely to say, "I want plenty of money" or "To be in shape," or even "Find love." Be definite as to the amount of money you want or what you want as possible. It's important.

2. Determine exactly what you intend to give or do, in return for what you desire.

3. Establish a definite date when you intend to possess your desire.

4. Create a definite plan for carrying out your desire, and begin at once, whether you are ready or not, to put this plan into action.

5. Write out a clear, concise statement of what you intend to acquire. Name the time limit for its acquisition, state what you intend to give in return for it and clearly describe the plan through which you intend to acquire it.

6. Read your written statement aloud, twice daily, once just before retiring at night, and once after waking in the morning.

This is an excellent method, especially if your affirmations are about personal gains. My example:

> I will earn $33,000,000 through sales related to my Foundations of Happiness purpose by 1 July 2019. I am going to invest my time and all my mental powers in it. I am writing my first book this year. I will use the money earned to fuel my passions for travel and to continue spreading my happiness mission.

The next method is my own and because of that it is my favorite.

1. Write an "I" statement about the desired improvement.

2. A "Why it's true."

3. A "What I intend to do with it."

4. An affirmative statement about achieving it.

> "I am a writer. I love the time I spend finding the perfect words and turn of phrase. I will schedule 30 minutes a day to focus on my writing. I have many books inside of me that people would love to read. Getting them out is going to be a labor of joy and love."

You can tweak the format to what works for you. Don't be afraid to play with the words a bit, until it sounds pleasant to your ear. They need to stir the passion that makes them worthy for you to say out loud each morning. You can have as few or as many as you can read in just a couple of minutes. I try to keep mine down to under a minute, when spoken aloud.

Once you have them written, you can read and review them at any time. The most critical part of this practice is saying them out loud twice a day with passion. The words themselves are just the vessel for your passionate desire of whatever it is you are after. Plain and unemotional reading of the affirmations will not make them the fantastic tool they should be. If you have something on your list of affirmations that doesn't naturally draw out strong emotion when said out loud, then you need to rewrite them or remove the ones that don't stir anything in you. This should be done once in the morning, and once in the evening, every day.

My current list of affirmations is presented below. I alter and tweak them regularly, as I achieve their intent. If any of my affirmations do not stir anything in you, I have provided you with some links to affirmation information and guides. I want you to succeed and if you find something else helpful online, drop me a link and share it with as many as possible.

My affirmations:

"I will no longer settle for less than the levels of success and fulfillment that I am truly capable of and deserve. In fact, I have a responsibility to live my life to the fullest and achieve my goals to set an example for those around me. To create the life I want, I can't wait for someday—or some year in the future. 'NOW is my time." ****I love this one, it sets the tone of my life. I borrowed some of it from Hal Elrod.

"I am a dedicated life partner and I am looking for the same! I am more than capable of satisfying a woman mentally, physically and emotionally. She will be silly and happy, cute and lively. She will help push me toward my goals, and I will push her toward hers. She is intelligent enough to recognize my mistakes, and strong enough to point them out to me. She is her own person, whose life I can make better and she mine. I am excited to meet her!"

"I like meeting new people and love hearing stories about their lives. When they ask me in return, I explain I live a completely charmed life. I will be an amazing friend to anyone who wants to invest their friendship in me."

"I am a writer. I love the time I spend finding the perfect words and turn of phrase. I will schedule 30 minutes a day to focus on my writing. I have many books inside me people would love to read. Getting them out is going to be a labor of joy and love."

"I will slay worry with action and fear with confidence. I will not imagine them to be larger than I am. After all, there is nothing to fear or worry about because I CAN NOT FAIL only learn and grow better."

"I will make my small part of the universe a better place for others. I will continue to think and act like the best person I can be and strive to be even better. Making the world better by teaching people how to be consistently happy is the purpose of my life. I am perfectly suited for this task. It is mine, and I will achieve it."

"I will earn $33,000,000 through sales related to my Foundations of Happiness Purpose by 1 July 2019. I am going to invest my time and all the mental power I possess into it. I am writing my first book this year. I will use the money earned to fuel my passions for travel and to continue my spreading happiness mission."

Napoleon Hill on auto-suggestion:
http://www.sacred-texts.com/nth/tgr/tgr09.htm

5 Steps to Make Affirmations Work for You by Ronald Alexander Ph.D:
https://www.psychologytoday.com/blog/the-wise-open-mind/201108/5-steps-make-affirmations-work-you

A different look and much shorter type of affirmation, great article, and good tips:
https://www.mindtools.com/pages/article/affirmations.htm

Even wikihow has a way to do it, and they did a great job! Illustrated and everything:
http://www.wikihow.com/Write-an-Effective-Affirmation

Why should I do it?

Choice is a human happiness need. Feeling stripped of options or the ability to steer our own life, defeats our will to actively participate. There have been many studies conducted in nursing homes about the patients being able to choose basic things. They have found the power to choose things like when to wake up, when to eat, when to call loved ones and where plants should be in their room, made enormous improvements in their patients' lives. Over a five year period, one study found that those given basic choices, complained far less, had fewer illnesses and even had a significantly lower rate of death.

Giving these elderly people back some simple control and choice makes a major improvement in their lives. This isn't a mystery to anyone who has ever felt like they did not have an option. Many people feel the same way about their emotional well-being. They feel like it is not theirs to dictate and they should suffer or enjoy it as it happens. If you are currently drowning in that river of emotion, it is time to choose to swim. If you put forth the effort to get where you want to be, maintaining it will be as easy as it was to float there.

Affirmations have been studied for their effectiveness numerous times in the last ten years. What they have found from brain-scan studies to more objective studies about participant well-being, is that they work universally as a mood and outlook improver. The reasons are plentiful, ranging from Reticular Activating System (RAS) and how we filter the world, to incongruent belief shaping, to brain scans that show remarkable changes in our reward centers. These are all fascinating reads but ultimately not helpful information. The useful bit that they all agree on is that affirmations, when done and anchored to feeling, are a very effective way to change your life for the better. Since willpower is a finite resource within us, our affirmations ease the required amount that we need to use each day.

There is not a hard choice on whether or not to write for me today. I have already chosen to do it. Following through takes far less willpower than deciding whether or not to do something. Affirmations also teach us to expect good things out of our day, "I will make my small part in this universe a better place for others." There is no question in my mind that I will do so.

My Story:

I was undergoing some huge changes in my life, when I found and started using affirmations regularly. I was preparing to retire with no job on the horizon and in a foreign county where job searching in the U.S. wasn't easy to do. I was also approaching the end of my divorce process. I hit a bump in my ability to remain positive. I wasn't depressed or even sad. It was just that maintaining a happy outlook started to get harder to do every day.

I knew I was struggling with everything and the stress was making it more difficult. I started looking for something to help me out. While I continued to search, I decided to tell myself "Today is going to be a great day!" I searched that phrase, and the first thing that came up was a video by The Lonely Island. It made me laugh through those first few days of saying the affirmation out loud. I would wake up and sing "I don't know why but today feels like it's going to be a great day!" and then laugh at the memory of the video.

I had such great luck those first few days. It also jogged a memory about affirmations. I went on the hunt for information relating to them. It took me five days to go from an idea to a list of affirmations that I used daily. I would write them, give them a test drive and then alter them, as needed. They made a significant difference in my ability to claim my happiness.

They also helped jump start my day into something more productive. They remind me each day the direction I want my life to go in, that I am worth my own effort, and point out the priorities I've set in my life. It is so effective that I started thinking of the reading of my affirmations as "Claiming my Happiness" for the day. I have continued to use them every day since. I've adapted and changed what I learned until I came up with what I have presented to you.

They work. Once written, they only take a minute or two to impact your entire day. Using them, from the simple one-word version to the short paragraph, can take your life to new heights. It is through these affirmations that I have been able to focus my life on being a better person and gained the motivation necessary to write this book.

The affirmations were a stepping stone into learning more about living in the present moment. As I have mentioned before, living in the present, sometimes called mindfulness, has been a happiness fueling machine for me. Learning to quiet unwanted, sometimes harmful thoughts, frees me to see and experience so much more. I do my best writing, flying and instructing from this state and have never experienced anything less than joy, when I find myself there.

After I started regularly seeking that state, it became easier to find it in almost any situation. I feel lucky to have been given the opportunity to find this quiet inner voice that pushes me to be better in the moment. I am certain that it is a step toward being a better me.

CHAPTER SEVEN

Into Action

HAPPINESS IS THE foundation of all the success in our lives. You shouldn't make the mistake of believing that only when you are successful will you find happiness. As we've discussed, you must choose the actions, emotions and thoughts that promote happiness in order to make claiming it effortless every day. Only then can success be achieved naturally and easily in any area of your life. Dispel the lie that happiness can only be achieved through the completion of our goals. Building happiness is the first step to greater life achievement. We can weather the trials of success and failure and never have to rebuild ourselves from the ground up if things go wrong. It is time to forgive yourself and accept the situation you are presently in. Tell yourself you are the person you want to be, visualize it and set goals so that you are able to achieve it. Find your purpose and follow it. That is how we will become happier and make our world a better place.

We have looked at the what's, how's and the why's, now let's talk about how to design your day to fit it all together. Some of these tasks naturally fit well in certain parts of the day, such as affirmations. Others you will need to look at your life and where they fit best. They all need a spot in your schedule to help keep you on track. There is no question that you have the time to do it all. It works with any schedule, because of how little time it takes to do most of the exercises Planning your day and including the new habits you have learned from this book, will help keep you on track.

For example: –

- Smiling takes no additional time in your day. You should smile every time you look in a mirror, just look at yourself because you are awesome! After you've practiced a few times and started using it, you'll notice what a powerful tool it is in shaping your happiness. [Chapter 1]

- Positive spin becomes second nature after some initial brain training. Therefore, it doesn't take any time out of your day either. [Chapter 3]

- Avoiding time devouring monsters like the blame game, self-pity and the ultimate time killer of negative thinking. This frees you and creates more time to achieve your goals. [Chapter 3]

- The very first thing you should do in the morning, before getting out of bed, is to make your first claim on happiness. "Today is going to be a great day!" or an awesome day or stupendous, whichever you prefer. [Chapter6]

- While getting dressed and having breakfast, think about something to feel grateful for. It can be anything that gives you a great, positive feeling. Scare the guy next to you with your outward declarations of gratitude, if necessary. This can include things like: I am grateful for the roof over my head. I am grateful for my job, (even if it could be a little more fulfilling.) It could even be: I am grateful for the supreme glory of waffles!

- Goals - I recommend reviewing your goals every Sunday. You should write a note about what you need to do each day for the coming week. Just put a sticky note on the bottom of your affirmations. If you are using a website to keep your affirmations, then create a Monday-Tuesday-etc. list at the bottom and update it once a week. This will allow you to do your daily affirmations and goal reviewing at the same time. They won't take more than a total of two or three minutes.

- At this point, I again recommend meditations. I truly believe in this amazing and life changing daily practice. Although it is not necessarily the main exercise that will bring you lasting happiness, I believe it makes the rest of the process smoother.

- Journaling about all the positive, negative and happiness you have experienced is something you can do at the beginning or the end of each day. I like to journal while I drink my morning tea. Give yourself a time limit in the morning since it can be easy to lose track when writing. It's a great way to start your day on the right foot.

- The only other component that we discussed, which does need to be done at a specific time, is the nighttime proclamation about the following day.

  "Tomorrow is going to be super great!"

- I have skipped forgiveness. Even though it is vitally important to give yourself the solid foundation through forgiveness and acceptance, you will only likely have to put effort into this once and then rarely afterwards. Accepting your current truth is a situational event that you will need to use one time.

- The other tools require no special time of the day, so bring out your dozens of smiles, multiple reward sessions with others, self-improvement, the chance to help, notice opportunities to use positive spin, and start living in the present moment.

All the things we have discussed are easy, require no special equipment, and they don't require any long training schedules to start using them. You can do them. They do work. Your belief will make them the most efficient habits you have ever used to live with happiness as your normal state of being.

As we come to the end of our journey, I'm going to give you an example of a typical day in my life. I hope this helps you. Please feel free to use it as part of your own daily structure. If it gets you to improve your life, then I have achieved what I set out to do.

- First, when I wake up, I smile big and say out loud "Today is going to be a great day!" It takes one second.

- While boiling the water for my tea, I meditate for 15 minutes.

- I get a pot of tea brewing and bring up and read my affirmations. It takes a total of three minutes.

- While I finish making my first cup of tea, I think about something to be grateful for and let myself feel thankful. This takes a total of two minutes.

- I review my goals for the day and prioritize what needs to be done. Since I do this daily, most days it only takes a minute.

- I use a minute or so to look at my vision board.

- I then sip tea and journal for 10 minutes.

This process takes a little less than a half an hour. If you are honest with yourself, you probably use the same amount of time to surf all of your social media accounts, while drinking your tea or coffee. Therefore, why not use this half an hour in a more active and inspiring way during your morning routine.

On my way to work, I practice being present and living in the moment. I then continue with this practice many times during the day. It is a super quick thing to do. It never adds any extra time to anything that I do. It just makes the things that I do go better.

I implement everything that we have talked about into my day. In the morning, I attempt to get everything on the priority goal list done. When I get to lunch, I spend at least 10 minutes of my lunch break reading something relating to self-improvement. I reward myself and put a positive spin on anything that impacts my life. This routine is now a part of who I am. Since I do it with ease, it adds nothing to my daily work schedule. The whole process just makes my day better with no added time.

After work, I hit the gym or the trail every other day. I also blog about happiness, mentor and coach those that need guidance and write for at least 30 minutes a day.

I have been on the road so long now, that most of my giving happens with charities I believe in or people that look like they need my help. All of these extra activities I do not only make my life better but are also stepping stones to achieving my life's purpose of spreading happiness.

The last thing I do after I crawl into bed, is claim my happiness for the next day. I claim my happiness with this phrase and it hasn't let me down yet.

"Tomorrow is going to be a super great day!"

I hope that everything I have shared with you has helped you to realize that happiness is within your grasp. You are in control of your happiness and destiny. There is nothing that can impact your happiness unless you let it. You will have bad days where you will struggle to dig deep and locate that happiness. That is OK. At the end of the day, we are only human. What I hope I have given you is a way to make sure that the happy days outshine the gloomy ones.

ABOUT THE AUTHOR

LEE E ELLIS is a combat veteran, a helicopter instructor pilot, a father, and crusader for personal happiness. Even in the test beds of combat and teaching people to fly complicated machines Lee has always found reasons to bounce back, keep smiling and a happy outlook. The ability to do so wasn't one he was born with but one taught to him by his father and then honed through education, trial and error, and research into the topic of happiness. After years mentoring fellow service members on how to maintain positive attitudes in difficult situations he decided to branch out and become an author. Lee's attitude toward the project is hopeful. If it helps one person, it will be worth the effort.

www.ingramcontent.com/pod-product-compliance
Lightning Source LLC
Chambersburg PA
CBHW061145040426
42445CB00013B/1563